GW00646527

Corporate collapse

the causes and symptoms

Also from McGRAW-HILL Book Company (UK) Limited

Mazzolini	European Transnational Concentrations
Frank	Organization Structuring
Denning	Corporate Planning
Duerr	Management Kinetics
Wilson	Financial Control

Corporate collapse

the causes and symptoms

John Argenti

McGraw-Hill Book Company (UK) Limited

London · New York · St. Louis · San Francisco · Auckland · Bogotá
Düsseldorf · Johannesburg · Madrid · Mexico · Montreal · New Delhi
Panama · Paris · São Paulo · Singapore · Sydney · Tokyo · Toronto

Published by McGRAW-HILL Book Company (UK) Limited
Maidenhead · Berkshire · England

07 084469 0

Library of Congress Cataloging in Publication Data

Argenti, John.
Corporate collapse.
Bibliography: p.
1. Bankruptcy. 2. Corporations. I. Title.
HG3761.A73 332.7′5 76–982
ISBN 0–07–084469–0

234 AP 7987

Printed and bound in Great Britain

Contents

Acknowledgements

I wish to express my sincere thanks to Miss Dare, the librarian at the British Institute of Management and to Miss Jones, the librarian of the American Management Association, for their help in tracking down books and articles on failure. My thanks are certainly also due to Professor Altman who helped me so liberally with chapter 4 and to all the experts who allowed me to take up so much of their valuable time when I was preparing chapter 3.

Exhibits 4.1 and 4.2, on pages 59 and 60, and the equations on pages 53 and 55, are reproduced by kind permission of Lexington Books, from *Corporate Bankruptcy in America*, by Edward Altman, and Exhibit 5.1, on page 84 is reproduced from Appendices 1 and 2, Rolls Royce Ltd (Investigation under the Companies Act 1948) by kind permission of the Controller of Her Majesty's Stationery Office.

1. *A proper subject*

Collapsed, failed, bankrupt, broke and bust. None of these are pleasant words, and this is not a very pleasant subject, but in real life companies do collapse, they do fail, do 'go bust'. And yet, how often does one see these words in books or articles on management? Hardly ever—it is most extraordinary. It is not only books: one cannot attend a lecture on the causes of failure as one can on every other conceivable management topic; one cannot consult an expert on the subject for there are virtually none.

This book is written in the belief that corporate collapse is a proper subject for study. The purpose of making the study is plain and simple. It is to try to learn what it is that causes perfectly healthy companies to collapse. If we can understand this mechanism perhaps we could then find some way of preventing their collapse or alleviating it or maybe even reversing it.

If this is a worthy aim, as I hope it is, why has no systematic study of the subject been made before? Throughout the past few decades the accent in management literature and in research has been upon the achievement of success. Inspect any book, any article in a journal or a newspaper, and you will see such titles as, 'The New Management: purposeful expansion' or 'Managing for results' or 'Dynamic growth'. You will not see, 'Symptoms of failure' or 'Causes of collapse'. Indeed, you will not find the words insolvency or Receiver or liquidation in the index of even such publications as guides to accountancy and finance for managers. Nor is failure exactly the central theme in the writings of that great management guru, Peter Drucker.

For decades now, the accepted criterion by which a company has been judged was how fast it has grown or how rapidly it has increased its share of the market or how many more employees it has now than it had before. It was surely right for growth to be considered the prime criterion then and it is right now and it probably always will be. Yet it can never have been right for this emphasis on success to have been so gross as to exclude completely every thought of failure and every thought of the terrible consequences of failure. It could never have made sense to shower praise upon a manager whose company succeeds yet when it fails to let him blame the government or workers or 'just bad luck'. The avoidance of failure has always been as much a part of a manager's task as the achievement of success. It has always been, it is more so now and will be more so still in the future, for the penalties for failure are becoming ever more severe.

Not only is the business environment becoming more hostile and risky and competitive, thus making failure more probable, but the growing reliance of people upon companies makes failure increasingly reprehensible. People will not accept failure as placidly as they used to; some will go to any lengths to avoid it. They organize sit-ins and protest marches, they call on the government for help. They will not even accept the collapse of a company providing cheap holidays abroad, so their response to the failure of a company providing something involving life and limb can only be imagined. No, today failure is not acceptable.

Corporate collapse has always brought fearful mental pain to proprietors and entrepreneurs and managers and to their families. It has always meant that employees lose their jobs, shareholders lose their savings, creditors lose cash and future business. The customer is deprived of the product. The local community may be plunged into despair. Failure has always brought years or decades of legal wrangling in its wake. It ruins lives, destroys the health of its victims; it pushes them to the edge of suicide and beyond. It has always been so but each individual in our modern society is becoming so much more dependent upon companies and other organizations that the misery of failure is now spread far and wide.

I do not wish to overstress the pain of failure, but I do wish to contrast the almost conspiratorial silence that surrounds the existence of failure and its consequences with the brash and blaring self-congratulatory ballyhoo that so often greets success. For too long managers and writers on management have shown the tourist the new and sparkling city centre, so to speak, and carefully kept him away from the slums and shanty towns. I would like to say again: the avoidance of failure is as much a part of a manager's job as the achievement of success.

If a manager wishes to learn the rudiments of business finance, or the details of a sales incentive scheme, or the principles of merger planning, or the mathematics of linear programming, he may consult a dozen different books, attend a dozen different lectures, consult a dozen different experts. If he wishes to know about failure and its symptoms or causes, its prevention or cure, his choice is negligible. There are a few books, some now rather out of date, and a few articles, most of which consist of lists of causes and symptoms. Some of what is stressed in one book is ignored in the others. Much of what is firmly stated in a book by a journalist is contradicted by an accountant; an academic says one thing, everyone else says another; few of the items in one list also appear in any other. While everyone agrees that bad management is the prime cause of failure no one agrees what 'bad management' means nor how it can be recognized except after the company has collapsed—then everyone agrees how badly managed it was.

And yet, as will be seen later, a great deal is known about corporate collapse; all that is missing from this neglected subject is for someone to pull it all together.

Just to do that would be helpful; but it would be even more useful if, having brought the pieces together, some of them could be fitted into a pattern. Thus the beginnings of a *coherent* body of knowledge on the subject of corporate collapse would be formed. A new management subject would be born.

Consider, for example, how useful it would be if we discovered that there was always one element present in every case of collapse; thus a manager has only to avoid it and he avoids failure! Or that there were three such elements; avoid them and he avoids failure. Of course, if it turned out (as fortunately it does not) that there are 87 such culprits, very little would have been achieved.

The dimensions of failure

In Britain approximately 600 000 companies are registered at the Department of Trade—the precise figure at the end of 1973 was 637 648. Of course, not all of these were trading, but the figure nevertheless astonishes many people whose concept of the number of companies in Britain is conditioned by the list of share prices published in daily newspapers. Most such lists contain a few hundred names (of which only a few dozen are known to the man in the street) and the number of public companies is only 17 000—a mere three per cent of all registered companies. In America there are 4½ million companies, approximately eight times as many as in Britain, which has approximately one quarter of America's population. Now, out of Britain's 600 000 companies approximately 8000 were 'dissolved' in 1973—that is 1·3 per cent. In America approximately 15 000 'fail' each year—that is less than 0·4 per cent. But we must *not* jump to any conclusions whatever, for not only is the definition of the word 'dissolved' different from the word 'fail' but the UK and US definition of 'company' is different too. So no comparison of failure rates is possible.

Now, whatever the definitions are, the fact is that apparently the number of failures compared with the number of going concerns is minuscule—one company in a hundred, probably. But look at these figures: over the five years 1969–74 the average number of companies on the British register was 586 000. The average number of new registrations each year was 43 000—or 7 per cent of companies registered. The average number dissolved *and* struck off was 26 000—or 4½ per cent. We do not know why these 26 000 companies disappeared each year; we know that 'dissolved' means that they ceased to exist as legal entities and we know that 'struck off' means that they were removed from the register for any of a dozen reasons including that the Registrar could get no reply to his letters to them.

The comparable figures for America are, approximately, that nearly 10 per cent of companies registered are new ones while nearly 9 per cent are removed from the register each year. These figures, like those for Britain, are surprising in two respects; the turnover of companies is far higher than most people realize—7 to 10 per cent new and 4½ to 9 per cent retiring—and the number of companies listed as having failed is much lower than most people expect—0·4 to 1·3 per cent. On the other hand, these low figures reflect official definitions of liquidation or dissolution only. They do not reflect the fact, as we must presume it to be, that most of those other companies that did not officially fail but which were nevertheless struck off the register, were unsuccessful ventures. If they had been successful they would not, one may presume, allow their continued existence to be jeopardized by being struck off an official register.

So what is the extent of failure? Is it as low as 0·4 per cent or as high as nine per cent—or somewhere in between, say three per cent? We do not know. Furthermore we will never know unless we most carefully define what we mean by 'failure' or 'collapse'. Before returning to consider these statistics, then, let us turn to these definitions.

Few of these definitions can be completely accurate; it is difficult to draw hard and fast lines and not always desirable. The most definitive words are *insolvent*, *liquidation*, *receivership* and *bankrupt*. In Britain companies do not go bankrupt (that is a term reserved for *people* only), they become 'insolvent' which means they cannot pay their debts as they fall due or that their net assets are of negative value. It is an offence to continue to trade while insolvent and directors and others who do so are liable to severe penalties. Instead, the bank usually calls in a 'Receiver' who takes over the management of the company and then does one of two things. He either continues trading, with the permission of the creditors and others, in the hope of bringing the company, or parts of it, round to profitability again, or he puts it into 'liquidation' which means the company stops trading and all its assets are sold for the benefit of the creditors. Those are the easy definitions.

Unfortunately these easy words are not the ones that interest us. Insolvency—and still more, liquidation—are the end points of the process of failure. They are the legal buffers at the end of the line. What interests us is how a company gets on to the failure track. That gives us a clue to a useful definition of collapse: collapse is when a company, which has hitherto been operating successfully, first begins to falter and then has to fight to remain profitable. Rolls-Royce certainly collapsed when its profits fell from £16m in 1968 to a loss of £12m two years later. Douglas Aircraft's shares fell from a value of $112 to $30 in six months. But collapse does not have to be sudden and dramatic, it can take years or decades. The key element is the transformation from corporate health and prosperity to a struggle for survival. It is the riches to rags story that we are concerned with here not the rags to riches story of most books on management.

But what about the word 'failure'? I shall use the word failure (or fail, failing, etc.) to refer to a company whose performance is so poor that sooner or later it is bound to have to call in the receiver or cease to trade or go into voluntary liquidation, or which is about to do any of these, or has already done so. Note that a company can be a failure without ever having been a success but it can only collapse if it was once successful but now is not.

The statistics I quoted above now come a little closer into focus. The number of companies that are put into liquidation each year in Britain is 8000. The number that fail is between 8000 and 26 000—but there is a strong hint that the figure is nearer the latter than the former because most people who have a successful company on their hands would not allow its registration to lapse. But we have no idea how many companies collapse each year nor how many companies there are which, having collapsed have not yet been liquidated nor how many there are which, having never succeeded are failing but not yet insolvent. I will make a guess: I suggest that 20 000 of the 26 000 companies that are removed from the register each year are failures. (The remainder, I am guessing, lapse in spite of being successful.) I also suggest that the process of failure takes 2½ years (I adduce some evidence for this later on) and so the number of companies that have collapsed or are in failure in any average year is 50 000 or, say, 10 per cent of all companies. My guess, then, is that if one examines any list of companies in Britain (and America, too, I assume) one in ten would be seen to be in failure, i.e., their profitability is so poor that they are bound to become insolvent within an average of 2½ years.

I cannot refrain from making the point again that, bearing in mind the terrible consequences of failure and bearing in mind that something like one company in 10 may be a failure, or at the very least not a success, the past neglect of this subject is most strange.

In the second issue of *Business Ratios* in 1969, R. Brough analyses the figures involved in the compulsory winding up, in 1965, of 100 companies. It appears that 82 per cent of these had been operating in three categories of business; building and contracting (30 per cent), distribution (29 per cent) and manufacturing (23 per cent). Over half the wound-up companies had a share capital of £100 or less and three-quarters of them were under £1000. Of the 52 which had the £100 share capital, no less than 16 had debts exceeding £10 000! Again, all seven companies in the £1000–£2000 capital category had debts exceeding £5000. It seems the creditors are the big losers.

Infant mortality is more common than senility, it appears. A quarter of Brough's 100 failed companies were wound up within two years; 62 were wound up in less than five years and only 21 had survived more than 10 years. As to the causes of failure, there seems to be some difference of opinion between the official Receiver and the managers of the failed companies (just as there is, noted above, between journalists, academics, accountants and managers). The official Receiver says the cause was 'mismanagement and gross mismanagement' in 71 out of 100. Of these, 51 had too little capital, five were due to inadequate accounting systems, and seven to excessive withdrawal of funds by directors. The managers agreed about too little capital being a major cause, but blamed bad debts in 18 cases, lack of experience in 10, poor labour or poor supervision in 10, keen competition in nine—but 'mismanagement' did not appear at all.

Brough notes that there is often a most rapid deterioration in the last year of failure and that at the start of this period many companies already have a deficiency of assets over liabilities so the creditors are at risk from then on. He comments that the proprietors may well carry on long after they should have stopped because they know that their own capital has already been lost. I should add two warnings: the sample Brough was working with was small—only 100 companies—and biased, in the sense that they were companies that had been subject to a compulsory winding-up. Of all the companies that fail each year (20 000?) only 1000 are compulsorily wound up. My second warning is that most of Brough's companies were very small. But then most companies are.

Diagnosis and treatment

My aim in this book is to bring together in one place an extensive collection of knowledge and experience on the early identification of failure and its prevention or cure. That this is worth doing has, I hope, already been demonstrated by the estimates, admittedly not much better than informed guesses, of the incidence of failure and by the undoubted fact that failure causes misery far beyond these figures. But there are a number of other important reasons for wishing to gain greater control over business failure today. One reason is the growing practice for employees to take a shareholding in their company; if it fails they lose their savings as well as their job. Another, valid only for the next few years, is that a great number of companies have been most severely damaged by the unusually severe economic downturn in 1974–5 and will remain highly vulnerable to failure for a number of years. Many will probably become finally insolvent during the next economic recession which, if it runs true to the four to five year cycle, will be in 1978–80.

Another reason is the growing size of companies. When they fail they either cause widespread damage or absorb enormous subsidies. Another is the doubts now widely held concerning the mechanisms of the capitalist system of which failure is one important part, acting rather as Darwin's survival-of-the-fittest mechanism acts, as a device for weeding out the weaklings. There must be growing doubt whether failure always now comes to weaklings and whether only weaklings fail.

What we need, then, is a coherent framework in which the causes of failure are set out, the symptoms listed and the ground-rules for diagnosis are laid down. We need to know what is the likely course of failure, what is the prognosis for the severity and duration of the illness. Is it always fatal once certain dreaded symptoms appear or can every company be saved? We need to know what treatment there is, whether a cash injection helps here or surgery there. Perhaps above all we need to know what preventative medicines there are and what healthy companies should do and not do to stay healthy. (Analogies are dangerous, as everyone knows, but the medical analogy with companies is often used; the 'company doctor', for example. The Receiver is often likened to an undertaker—a comparison that is now highly inaccurate—see p. 31.)

I think it will be seen that all these questions are answered in the last three chapters, that these answers are very definitive and of quite remarkable practical value. I hope and believe that they are on an altogether new plane to some of the books and articles published on this subject. I shall describe a number of these books in later chapters—indeed I must make it clear that almost all the material on which my conclusions are based comes from other people's first-hand knowledge or published work—but I would like to discuss one typical article on failure here in order to examine certain defects that I shall try to avoid when we come to construct our own list later.

This article appeared in the *Financial Times* on 9 November 1973 and described a list of failure symptoms in small businesses, compiled by Mr Robert D. Bullock, a consultant in San Francisco. His first item is 'lack of any plan—the company just reacts to events'. Second, there is such a shortage of cash that the company cannot pay the wages unless a big cheque from a customer comes in. Then: morale is low, profits are low because sales are weak or costs are higher than expected, there is late delivery, low stock turnover, poor or late management information, loss of orders from customers, a lot of executive overtime, pricing by guess-work. . . . But stop!

Stop and ask what Mr Bullock is doing here. It looks as though he has merely written down, in no particular order related to importance or to the sequence of their appearance, all the symptoms of failure he has ever seen in a sick company. He has not distinguished between causes of failure and symptoms (lack of planning may be a cause, not a symptom; not being able to pay the wages may be a symptom, not a cause). He has not distinguished between the symptoms you only see in sick companies and those you can observe in healthy ones too. I feel strongly that these are vital defects. The need to distinguish between cause and symptom is obvious; if one wishes to reduce the chances of failure one might do so by adopting a lot of planning, thus removing a cause of failure. But it would be ineffective, not to say meaningless, to try to stop failure by having enough cash to pay wages!

Again, if one was walking through one's factory or office and saw a lot of executives working overtime, or late delivery to customers, or poor management information, one would not be justified in concluding that one's company was failing. But not enough cash to pay the wages—now you would!

Let us now look at the next few items in his list: excessive scrap ratios, too much reworking, desks piled high with paperwork. And I could add a hundred more: lorry breakdowns, high labour turnover, offices need repainting, wastepaper baskets need emptying. . . . These are completely useless because one can also observe them all in companies that are not failing. Surely there are some symptoms and some causal agents or some preconditions, proclivities or predispositions which are seen singly or in certain combinations *only* in companies that are going to fail? I think it will become clear that there are (one or two of them are, in fact, present in Bullock's list above but buried under a weight of irrelevant chaff).

This, then, is the aim of this book. To put into the hands of managers and accountants, shareholders and bankers, workers and civil servants, customers and creditors—as well as those currently useless watchdogs, the outside directors—a systematic body of knowledge about corporate collapse. I shall tackle the task in the sequence outlined below. First I have to mention the following conventions; I shall write m for million and bn for billion (1 000 000 000). I shall use the English word 'gearing', not the American equivalent 'leverage', and 'ordinary' and 'shares', not the American equivalent 'common' and 'stocks'.

In the next chapter I shall bring together the views of leading writers on failure. A consensus does emerge in spite of the fact that some of them are journalists, some are managers, some are accountants and all have their distinctive viewpoints. In the following chapter, chapter 3, I record the opinions of a dozen leading experts in failure. Many are professional Receivers, but there are investment analysts, managers and journalists too. Again, a consensus emerges, this time a more coherent one.

In chapter 4 I summarize the findings of the only really significant academic to be working in this field and I examine the equations he has developed which are designed to estimate a company's propensity to fail. In chapters 5 and 6 I recount in great detail two of the most important failures in recent economic history, Rolls-Royce and Penn Central, with the intention of testing out the conclusions reached in the earlier chapters. They pass the test with flying colours and a really clear picture of how companies enter the path of failure begins to emerge.

In chapter 7, on causes and symptoms, all the lessons of the previous chapters are listed under thirteen headings. By now it becomes clear that this is not *just* a list of causes and symptoms, such as those put forward by Bullock and others, but it has its own dynamic. It is more a film of the process of failure than an album of thirteen snapshots. In chapter 8 we discover that we have, in fact, three films—or rather, that we have the story-line of three different failure-paths each of which is followed by only one type of company. Thus, very young, small companies follow one distinctive failure-path; young larger companies follow another equally distinctive path which includes a period of dramatic collapse; finally, mature companies follow a rather complex three-stage failure-path.

In chapter 9 these conclusions as to causes and symptoms and paths of failure are used to suggest a number of most important measures for preventing failure in the three types of company and, where appropriate, for their rescue from failure. Consideration is given to some of the measures that might be taken by governments, banks, managers, shareholders and stakeholders.

It is necessary to utter a warning here, which I shall repeat at occasional intervals throughout the book. So far as I know this is the first serious attempt to bring order into the subject of corporate collapse. It is not the last word, it is the first. As such it will be imperfect and, although I now feel a considerable sense of confidence in my conclusions, it would be naïve in the extreme for anyone blindly to diagnose failure of a given company just because it displays some superficial similarity with my descriptions of failure. A misdiagnosis, especially a published one, could cause severe and wholly unnecessary damage to a company. It would be equally naïve for anyone blindly to apply my proposed remedies. Great care and even delicacy is required not to do more harm than good.

2. *What the writers say*

There are few serious writers in this field. The fashion in management literature for the past two decades has been to concentrate on go-go performance and how to achieve it. While it was right that this should be so, and it still is, it is nevertheless extraordinary that so little should have been written about failure and how to avoid it. The one really serious and advanced writer on failure is Professor Altman and I shall devote the whole of chapter 4 to his work. In this chapter I shall summarize a number of books on failure—almost all of them by journalists—together with a number of articles from financial newspapers and management journals. Journalists often tell these tales of business failure extremely well. Although they seldom reach conclusions, are often superficial and even inaccurate, yet, taken together, some very interesting lessons do emerge from their stories. But I shall start by summarizing one of the few books on failure that is not written by a journalist.

Ross and Kami

One would think from the somewhat racy title of their book, *Corporate*

Management in Crisis: Why the Mighty Fall, that these two authors were journalists. Joel E. Ross and Michael J. Kami have both had practical management experience, however. Their most general conclusion is that the cause of failure is bad management, and in particular the breaking of Ten Commandments. It is worth listing these:

1. You must have a strategy and must communicate it.
2. You must have overall controls and cost controls.
3. The board must actively participate.
4. Avoid one-man rule.
5. Provide management depth.
6. Keep informed and react to change.
7. The customer is king.
8. Do not misuse computers.
9. Do not engage in accounting manipulations.
10. Provide an organization structure that meets people's needs.

Ross and Kami go through each of these in turn illustrating how each commandment has been broken by one well-known firm after another. There is no lack of examples but I am less than convinced by some of their arguments. They say that IBM has a strategy and so IBM has not collapsed, while Lockheed's strategy was ill-chosen and so Lockheed has collapsed; but Lockheed did *have* a strategy and, as Ross and Kami admit, it was seen to be at fault only in retrospect. Again, they say that Rolls-Royce failed because it did not have a strategy; but my impression is that Rolls-Royce very definitely did have a strategy (see chapter 5) but it too was seen to be faulty in retrospect. They also say that Rolls-Royce failed because they misused computers; but I cannot see anything in the Official Report about this and my impression was that Rolls were rather good with computers, numerically controlled machine tools, and so on.

Again, take their Fourth Commandment. They say that Jim Ling (of LTV), Bernie Cornfeld (of IOS), Darryl Zanuck (of 20th Century Fox), and Saunders (of Penn Central) are examples of one-man bands which collapsed. But they also list these men as corporate heroes: Walt Disney, Tom Watson (of IBM), David Sarnoff (of RCA) and Harold Geneen (of ITT). So I am left wondering whether one-man rule is a good thing or a bad, and how to draw the line between them in real life. But I also ponder these thoughts; was Penn Central a one-man band? I did not think so (see chapter 6). Is Harold Geneen still a corporate hero? The value of ITT's shares has collapsed since Ross and Kami published in 1973—from around $60 in 1968 to $12 in 1974. If Geneen is still a hero in spite of this, does he still 'keep ITT on top by understanding synergism' as Ross and Kami claim for him?

Throughout this book, I felt, Ross and Kami were trying to find examples to illustrate their conclusions instead of the other way round. And I also felt that some important lessons were not included in the Ten Commandments. For example, Ross and Kami say that another reason that Rolls-Royce failed was that their board was unbalanced—engineers greatly outnumbered accountants. I agree. They say exactly the same about Lockheed. I agree. But surely this is such a common failing that it should appear among the commandments even if that makes them eleven! Cash flow control is not mentioned either. Twelve?

At the end of each chapter the authors list the lessons learned. These total 127, and while some of them come within the Ten Commandments some of them do not. Ross and Kami must have realized this because at the end of the book the Ten have risen to 23, which now also include operational planning, profit planning, marketing, hardening of arteries, management information systems, balance (ah, good!), conglomeration, employee progress, innovation, leadership and capital structure. (Still no cash flow, though.) Among the 127 dos and don'ts are: decentralize into small profit centres, avoid panic cost cutting, be wary of profit centres, cut the paperwork—and so on. Ross and Kami suggest that if you inspect a crashed company you will find that a number of things have been wrong; lack of control plus poor planning plus one-man rule plus misuse of computers and so on. I agree. But you will also find a number of things wrong in companies that have not collapsed. What we are trying to find out, not very successfully so far, is what are the *fatal* flaws. But the converse is true also. We could inspect a collapsed company and find that hardly any of Ross and Kami's commandments had been broken. What was wrong with Burmah Oil's operating planning, employee progress, marketing, management depth, etc., etc.? Nothing so far as I know.

I remain confused. I do not know now if there are 10 causes of failure or 23 or 127. Or, if you believe Barmash, only one—greed!

Barmash

There is no doubt in the mind of Isadore Barmash what causes collapse. This is how he starts his *Great Business Disasters*:

> Corporations are managed by men; and men, never forget, manage corporations to suit themselves. Thus corporate calamities are calamities created by men. And, as we shall see in fifteen case histories, the basic cause of the business disaster is greed, human greed, simple and unadulterated. In most cases, the greed crossed over the line into corruption.

Among his fifteen cases we meet such extraordinary people as Philip Musica, Billie Sol Estes and Anthony De Angelis on whose bubbling entrepreneurial endeavours some remarkable fortunes were built and lost. Barmash also describes what happened to William Zeckendorf, whose firm, Webb and Knapp was probably the largest real-estate company in the world. In 1965 it owned 8000 hotel bedrooms and was responsible for urban renewal projects of enormous proportions. Its collapse came when a super-enormous project called Freedomland (an amusement park) went wrong and the company failed owing $84m. But Zeckendorf is still around doing property deals, having settled with his creditors. Barmash particularly remarks on Zeckendorf's ability to persuade backers to put up money for his schemes. In fact one of the deepest impressions made throughout his book was the ability of all the various characters he describes to do this. Or, to put it the other way round, there seems to be a remarkable willingness on the part of backers to finance certain people's ideas.

This willingness is not limited to entrepreneurs at the fringes of the financial world, it appears to extend right into established banks and well-known financial institutions, most of whom have professional investment appraisal departments. Barmash tells us of the Atlantic Acceptance Corporation, for example, which began in hire purchase and other loan business on a small scale, grew rapidly, was backed first by a well-respected financier, grew further, was then backed by several leading Canadian and American banks, grew again and then, in 1965, collapsed. The cause was simple: the ever-increasing resources at its disposal necessitated growth; having lent money to everyone who could repay it, Atlantic Acceptance could only achieve more growth by lending to people who could not.

Another lasting impression from Barmash's book is that all these characters are cast in the same mould. They are super-salesmen, flamboyant, live life twice as fast as other people. Eddy Gilbert was another one. He too was a super-salesman and, like so many of them, rather short in stature. In 1958 he persuaded his friends to buy him a controlling share in a timber firm called E. L. Bruce. But having gained control the share value dropped and in 1962 the firm collapsed.

Bernie Cornfeld is another example. He had the brilliant idea of selling company shares direct to the public on hire purchase, and in 14 years his Investors Overseas Services grew to be worth $2 000 000 000. It employed 15 000 very well-paid salesmen. Its investment decisions swayed the world's stock markets. His downfall was due to several causes; some of IOS's investments were unsound; it was revealed that IOS directors had borrowed money from IOS; traditional bankers were alarmed at Cornfeld's flamboyance—dolly girls and financial probity are not in their eyes compatible.

Only two of Barmash's characters do not fit the super-salesman description. One is Stanley Goldblum, who was large and quiet and introspective. He was chief executive of Equity Funding Life Insurance Company which crashed in 1973. Its business was equity linked life insurance. I am not sure from Barmash's book whether Goldblum knew about it, but there was in Equity Funding an operation called Department 99. Their task was to invent names and addresses of 'clients', their date of birth and, of course their death, in order to provide additional 'cash flow' for the books. A large number of people in the firm knew, joked about it and helped to put the inspectors off the scent.

The other character is Robert Sarnoff. David Sarnoff (one of Ross and Kami's corporate heroes) had built up RCA on colour television and his son Robert wanted to carry on the growth through computers. But IBM dominated that industry and in the late sixties RCA had only three or four per cent of the market. So David decided on a policy of imitating IBM and undercutting them—Project Intercept it was called. When RCA launched its IBM-like computers, however, instead of taking business from IBM they took it from existing RCA computer customers. In money terms (though not I think in real terms) the loss of $400 million that RCA made on this abandoned project exceeded even Ford's loss on the Edsel.

Brooks

In his book *The Fate of the Edsel* John Brooks explains how, in 1955, Ford decided to introduce a new medium-sized car into their product range. In keeping with the then fashion, their stylist, Roy A. Brown, designed it long, low and wide, glistening with chrome, bristling with push buttons and redolent with horse power. But to distinguish it from other similar cars he stuck on some wings to add a little *je ne sais quoi*. The project manager, Krafve, suggested the car should be named after one of Henry Ford's sons, Edsel, but the family were not keen on this and a great campaign began to find a better name. Foote, Cone and Belding, the advertising consultants in Madison Avenue, suggested a shortlist of 6000 names—'Good God', said Krafve, 'we only wanted one.' A firm of pollsters interviewed the public. Marion Moore, the poet, was commissioned to put forward some imaginative ideas, one of which was 'Utopian Turtle Top'. Hundreds of possible names were printed on slides and projected in front of Ford executives in a darkened room (occasionally they were shown a slide with 'Buick' written on it to keep them awake). At last Krafve said, 'I don't like any of them. We'll call it Edsel.'

The launch took place in 1957 against a background of falling car sales and a falling stock market. Two other Ford divisions were having a special sales campaign. The Edsel itself proved to be dramatically imperfect: buttons didn't push, bits fell off, oil leaked generously. It became a joke. Within weeks it was clear that it was a failure and was withdrawn in 1959, for a loss of $350m.

Brooks believes there are several lessons here. First, it is unfair to blame Brown, the stylist, as so many people tend to do. Radical changes in taste took place between the time he designed it and its launch two years later. Second, it is unfair to blame an excess of psychology and motivational research methods. In the case of the name, at any rate, all these techniques were rejected when Krafve said, 'I don't like any of them. We'll call it Edsel.' Third, the Edsel may have gone but Ford has not. Huge though this project was, it was not so large that its failure would bring Ford down too. In fact Ford's shares stood at $60 in 1957, fell to $40 in 1958 and rose to $90 in 1959. Hardly even a dent! Fourth, none of the team working on the Edsel had the slightest warning that it was going to fail. There were no early symptoms before the launch.

This book is about company failure, so we are not really interested in product failures (like the 'Edsel' and 'Project Intercept') unless they are so great that they might cause the company to fail too. Let us look at a case in the construction industry where this happened, although, as will become clear, other things were wrong with the company as well.

Simmonds

In the February 1974 issue of *Management Today*, D. T. Simmonds describes how Mitchell Construction failed early in 1973. It left behind part of London's Fleet Line Underground, a hydroelectric scheme, and the Kariba power station, all unfinished. The story goes back to 1968 when David Morrell, its founder and chief executive, realized that the company was on a plateau and needed a boost. The ideal project came their way—a half share in the huge Kariba power station. Unfortunately their partner dropped out and Mitchell took on his share as well. Things went wrong: rockfalls, squabbles with other contractors, and so on. So payment was delayed and costs rose. But payment for other work was also being delayed. There was nothing very unusual about that because many of Mitchell's projects were complex and many governments and sub-contractors were involved, but by 1973 no less than £11m out of £40m annual turnover was in dispute and not paid in. Worse still, there was also a downturn in business.

Simmonds puts the blame firmly on Morrell. He says he did not decentralize as the company expanded; he did not bother with small projects, only with very big ones; he did not seek new areas of business to replace the falling demand for power stations in the UK; he should not have undercut into the Kariba projects; he did not have a management succession policy (all he had was a lot of committees); he did not have enough finance men. It was and remained for far too long a one-man band. (Strong confirmation for Ross and Kami's Fourth Commandment!)

Deeson

While on UK companies, let me describe some of the cases discussed by A. F. L. Deeson in his *Great Company Crashes* (not to be confused with Barmash's *Great Business Disasters*!). Deeson offers no summary and no conclusions but describes 10 failures. One of the most impressive is the City of Glasgow Bank (1839–78) because, among various other items contributing to the loss of £6m, one of the directors lent himself £2·3m—a century ago that represented a sum of money worth perhaps £20m today!

Deeson describes the Lanchester Engine Company (1896–1904) founded by a brilliant engineer who insisted on making every part of the famous Lanchester Car in his own works—no one else could meet his quality standards. It was this technical perfectionism that caused this collapse because they ran out of cash as a result of endless development costs. But the drop in sales due to the South African War did not help—nor did his board, who knew nothing about his company and took no interest in it. (See Ross and Kami's Third Commandment!)

Deeson then discusses Cyril Lord. Not only was Lord a powerful personality but his knowledge of the technology of carpet manufacture was unrivalled. He had made £1m in his first 10 years of business and then began his major expansion based on tufted carpets made in a huge factory in Ireland. Turnover in 1966 was £10·8m and profits £1·3m. His boundless energy then took him into making poplin in South Africa, artificial astrakhan, vinyl floors, Cyrilawn (a plastic grass), and sculptured carpets. He built a huge office block, a computerized carpet store, he opened wallpaper shops and carpet shops. Virtually all of these failed. For example, the carpet shops were too small in area to allow the salesmen to display the carpets to customers. Deeson says he had no management depth and no full-time finance director so that, for example, against Lord's forecast of £1·1m profit for 1968 they were really making a loss, and no one, not even Lord himself, knew it.

Now for John Bloom. He also was a man of boundless energy, of rather small stature, a super-salesman and he also had a brilliant idea. This was to sell washing machines to the increasingly better-off UK mass market not, as everyone else did, through the wholesale–retail chain with its enormous price mark-ups, but direct from factory to consumer. He advertised his machines in the local press at absurdly low prices and because of rapidly rising volume soon had to find his own production facilities in UK. He merged with Rolls Razor, who had a factory but no product, and sales boomed.

His boundless energy took him into cut price shops, Bulgarian holidays, Super Golden Trading Stamps, home movies, TV rentals. All were failures. His latest washing machine was a mechanical failure too. It all ended in 1964 with a £4m loss.

Finally, Deeson recounts the story of Dr Emil Savundra, who launched his insurance company, Fire, Auto & Marine, in England in 1963. So ruthlessly did he cut premiums that he obtained a significant volume of business; so much so that the insurance industry asked the UK government to investigate under their powers in the 1958 Companies Act. Their report said there was 'no immediate danger of insolvency'. One week later the Receiver was called in. If anyone needed evidence that the prediction of collapse is a difficult thing to do, there it is.

Smith

R. A. Smith's book is called *Corporations in Crisis* (not to be confused with Ross and Kami's *Corporate Management in Crisis*). Smith comes to several general conclusions. He believes that centralization is a wellspring of crisis and the central cause is the boss. Thus Henry Ford still ran the company himself long after it had passed the size that any human being could handle alone. He so far failed to change his methods that in 1946 he was still employing anti-union thugs, had no R&D and no cost control—just like 1920. Smith sees this failure to change fast enough as a potent cause of collapse; Luckenbach did nothing when railroads began to compete with their coastwise shipping; United Fruit did nothing when fruit juices challenged their bananas at breakfast; Baldwin-Lima-Hamilton did nothing when diesel locos threatened steam; Knox Glass did nothing when natural gas trumped their only ace—that their works was near coal. Curtis Publishing didn't do this, Curtiss Wright didn't do that . . . Smith gives plenty of examples.

His third potent cause is bad luck, as when, for example, Crane Company's six top men were all killed in an air crash, or the fire at Pontiac's factory. His fourth cause is decentralization; he lists Blaw Knox, Consolidated Freightways, General Electric and General Dynamics as examples of companies that delegated autonomy to subsidiaries without an adequate system of reporting performance. Fifth, he lists diversification as something that can cause collapse if it goes wrong. But he generalizes further: most causes of failure, he says, can be seen as either something done to excess or as something done feebly. (He rather spoils this by giving, as an example of feebleness, the lack of market research that caused the Edsel failure. John Brooks said that most people think they did too much!)

I think we will find these conclusions very useful even though this book was written at the height of the go-go performance craze by a journalist who delights in what I can only call the 'tough-minded hard-driving John Nash' style of writing. He also tends to exaggerate a little where he dwells at length on the crisis for Howard Hughes when RKO Studios lost several million dollars. Several million dollars is a crisis? For Howard Hughes?

Houston

Another attempt to list the signs of debility is Brian Houston's article in *Harvard Business Review* of November 1972. There are four main symptoms, he says. One is *espirit de corps*; people employed by successful companies feel they are in something special, they know where they are going, what they are doing (and just making money is not it) and are inspired by good leaders. All this is absent in the moribund company, often noticeably so. (I cannot disagree but I note sadly that morale, sense of direction and inspired leadership were very high indeed in the Edsel team under Krafve and at times in the RB 211 team. Both failed.)

Houston's second symptom is an ageing product; innovation is essential. His third is a sense of 'now'. But it is not only a sense of urgency that is lacking in sick companies, the managers there are always looking for crutches instead of opportunities. Finally, he says that an understanding of cash flow is vital. One must not confuse depreciation with profits and must be wary of obsolescence.

Cohen

Here is another list of symptoms. This is by David Cohen and appeared in *Business Administration* in January 1973 under the title 'Confidence comes before a crash'. His list includes the following:

1. Liquidity problems must be investigated—they may be signs of approaching disaster.
2. It is surprising how easily credit can often be obtained.
3. Make sure that your customer mix is not drifting towards the bad payers.
4. Keep abreast of technology.
5. Do not put prestige above profit.
6. Do not have too few customers.
7. You should ask why if your growth rate is not seven or eight per cent per annum.
8. Treat your employees as human beings.
9. Do not overexpand.
10. Do not borrow too much or at too high interest rates.

Cohen also notes that managers seldom seem to realize that they are on the verge of collapse until it actually happens.

It is a source of some amusement (and interest too) to see how different these lists are. It is already clear that one or two items come up frequently but it is surprising how many items do not recur. No one has confirmed Cohen's items 3, 5, 6 or 7, just as no one has confirmed Ross and Kami's commandments 5, 7, 8, 9 and 10. I am not rejecting any of these yet, merely noting that they do not recur. On the other hand 'Keep up with change' comes up like clockwork, as do a few others. Let us see what items there are on the next list.

Hartigan

P. W. J. Hartigan is an insolvency manager. He lists seven main causes of failure in an article called 'Causes of company failure' in *The Accountant* of 22 March 1973. First, there is *lack of capital.* In the early years of a business the proprietors often obtain assets on hire purchase, they seldom make allowances for early losses and so become highly dependent on the good will of creditors who do not always relish the role. Overtrading (rapid expansion in turnover not matched by an expansion of capital) is a frequent cause of failure especially where inadequate costing methods are used. Second, *undercosting*; often there is no costing system at all and, even where there is, such things as interest on loans or depreciation are forgotten. Third, *lack of control*; the proprietor prefers to be active himself rather than check up on other people's activities. Fourth, *lack of advice*; proprietors are reluctant to ask for advice from bankers, accountants, solicitors and so on. Fifth, *the government*; a great many bankrupts blame the government, but very often this is just an excuse—everyone knows that, without warning, tax rates change, laws are passed, credit is squeezed. Sixth, *trade fluctuations*; companies are often caught out by the business cycle, by mergers and by technological change. Finally, *fraud*; this cause is increasing.

Hartigan believes that greed, stubbornness and dishonesty are causes but the strangest thing is the proprietor's refusal or inability to see unpalatable facts. However, if success brings acclaim, surely failure should bring blame. He adds that his list of causes may seem obvious and elementary but this is the nature of truth. Well, let us test him. Let us now look at a case study of a real failure and see how many of Hartigan's seven can be seen; and let us at the same time look for evidence of Cohen's Ten, Houston's Four and Smith's Five!

Business Week

The collapse of a company called Stirling Homex is described in some detail in an article in *Business Week* of 28 October 1972. The story began in 1967 when two Canadian brothers, William and David Stirling, set up a company to manufacture factory-built modular homes. They were already in the building business in a modest way but most of the capital they needed came from a Mr Sibley, an experienced construction industry financier. Many of the first modules produced were used in a publicity stunt—they built a suburb of 275 homes in 36 hours! The company was greatly expanded in 1968 and the enlarged board included Mr Sibley and a stockbroker, whose expertise, plus some more publicity stunts by the brothers, led to a stock market quotation only two years after the company was formed. The shares, offered at $16.50, rose to $51.75.

There is little doubt that these two men (in fact it was mainly David) knew how to put on a show: they sent a 2000 ft-long train of modules to relieve a town hit by a hurricane. That attracted huge publicity. So did their demonstration of a method of building high-rise flats by jacking up the building and slipping another module in underneath. Huge orders were received and the factory was expanded. The big ideas brought big money, the big money brought big names: Peat Marwick the auditors, Merrill Lynch the brokers, Chemical Bank. . . . Then came *la dolce vita* in the form of executive jets, Lincoln Continentals, pretty secretaries. Output continued upwards but sales did not and so it became necessary to put the modules into stock; they were of course all sold on contract or if not actually on contract then the contract would be along any day so it was perfectly all right to enter them—about 9000 of them—in the books at the full sales value of about $35m. Not everyone was happy about these figures and eventually the end came as it had to and Stirling Homex filed for bankruptcy on 10 July 1972. Luckily for Chemical Bank and others they were not legally bound to their loans of $55m.

Well, how many items in those lists did you spot? If you saw as few as I did we should ask ourselves what has gone wrong for these lists are intended as distillations of knowledge about the process of collapse. It looks as though either we do not know much about it or Stirling Homex is an exception to the rule—but Stirling Homex seems to me to have a number of features in common with many of the other cases we have seen in this chapter such as those described by Barmash and Deeson. I believe we will only be able to reach a really useful practical set of conclusions if we study a number of failures (one or two of which we must look at in detail). Let me therefore summarize here, very briefly, a number of stories of failure that have recently appeared in the Press.

The Press

On 1 December 1973 the *Financial Times* described how, in 1961, Mr Gerald Caplan, a barrister, acquired control of London and Counties Securities Limited. Under his guidance this small private firm, acting as banker to supermarkets, advertising media, department stores and other elements in the modern consumer world, expanded rapidly. By 1969 its profits reached £180 000 and it went public. By 1970 its shares rose to 180p. L & C then made several acquisitions and moved into retail banking (i.e., it set up branches inside such large retail stores as United Drapery Stores which, incidently, was itself a substantial investor in L & C). Jeremy Thorpe, the Liberal Party leader, joined the board in 1971. By 1972 the shares touched 358p. The end was sudden and apparently caused by public annoyance over 'excessive interest rates' being charged by the company. Public opinion was strong enough to bring an inquiry by the Department of Trade and confidence in L & C evaporated.

On the same day, the *Financial Times* also described the failure of Piccadilly Estates. This London hotel company expanded very rapidly for some years and into 1973, which was the year when foreign tourists failed to appear in the numbers predicted. The occupancy level fell below breakeven and the cash, earmarked for hotel construction payments, ran out.

A few days later, the *Financial Times* published a detailed account of the failure of Geo. W. King. The story started many years ago when Donald King, an ideas man, a salesman and entrepreneur built the company on his skill in designing conveyor systems for motor manufacturers. But by 1965 the company was making losses and Donald, then 72, wanted to sell out. Tube Investments—one of the biggest UK engineering companies—bought it for £2m in 1971. But there was then a depression in the UK capital goods sector and no orders were received until 1972. It was then discovered that the market for the sort of package deal that Donald King was so good at was dying because by now the motor manufacturers were pretty good at it themselves. The thousand employees were moved elsewhere in TI and Kings ceased trading.

One of the strangest stories in 1974 was the £1m investment that Kleinwort Benson made in a large Japanese central heating company called Nihon Netsugaku Kogyo two weeks before it failed with debts of £95m. Again, if anyone needs proof of how difficult it is to predict failure, one needs only to remember that Kleinwort Benson are one of London's most respected merchant banks.

On 7 June 1974 *The Times* discussed the fall of Wilstar Securities, the company run by Mr William Stern. The story lasts a mere three years from when William Stern left the family business (in property) and launched out on his own into the then booming property market. He quickly obtained backing from several respected banks and rapidly acquired a number of companies including the well-known Key Flats and certain residential blocks. He expanded into industrial, office and shop development. As the industrial developments were completed he sold them to provide cash to pay the loan interest while retaining the other properties as collateral. Unfortunately three things, all connected, occurred: the market for industrial property declined, interest rates on short-term money —which is what he mainly had—increased, and the Labour government introduced a rent freeze. In spite of all this Mr Stern did not, according to *The Times*, draw in his horns early in 1974 and the crash came in June.

A few months later the property market collapse, which by now was world-wide, caused the failure of the construction and property company, Mainline Corporation in Australia. According to the *Financial Times* of 22 August 1974, Mainline began in 1960 and grew at a spectacular rate— indeed, it is generally agreed the rate was too spectacular and the level of borrowings, at 75 per cent of total capital, was too high. Among the other causes were the Labour government's tax and legislation programme (which was markedly anti-property), industrial disputes, the union ban on property development, inflation and high interest rates.

On 5 November 1974 the *Financial Times* told another story of labour disputes and rising costs in the construction industry. This one, concerning a 110-year-old private UK company called Cornes Tideswell, goes back a number of years to when inflation first started to push costs up but when most government agencies were still demanding a fixed price contract from building constructors. As to the industrial disputes, of course the management blame the unions and vice versa. A comment of the union's regional secretary was that things had gone wrong in the late 1950s when the company did not come to terms with modern labour employment practices.

Interim conclusions

Some of the writers whose views I have summarized in this chapter have put forward one or two ideas that have struck no chord with anyone else. I mentioned in chapter 1 Bullock's belief that 'desks piled with paperwork' was a sign of impending failure; no one else has mentioned this. No one else mentions Ross and Kami's 'Do not misuse computers' as a significant element in avoiding failure. No one except Smith has mentioned diversification as a potent cause.

On the other hand there certainly is widespread agreement on a number of key factors, which I will now list. Of course, it is an interim list only for it is based so far on the views of a handful of writers. But I think we already have a number of important pieces of the jigsaw puzzle.

TOP MANAGEMENT

Three of Ross and Kami's commandments are about management: avoid one-man rule, make sure the whole board participates, make sure there is management in depth. Simmonds notes the one-man rule of Morrell at Mitchell Construction, the lack of management depth there and the unbalanced board (not enough finance men). Deeson tells us of Lanchester's one-man rule and lack of participation by his board; and of Cyril Lord's one-man rule, no finance men, and no management depth. Smith reminds us of Henry Ford's one-man rule and no finance men. Almost all the Barmash stories are about one-man rule and so are London and County, King, Wilstar and Stirling Homex.

ACCOUNTING INFORMATION

Cohen and Hartigan both notice how so many bosses do not see (or are unwilling to see) the disaster ahead until it is upon them. This could be due to poor accounting information. Whether this is so or not, most of the writers mention lack of information and control as a major cause: Ross and Kami, Hartigan, Smith, Deeson, Houston, Cohen and Brough (in chapter 1). Some of them particularly mention one particular aspect—credit control, for example, or costs, or cash flow. Oddly enough, none of

Barmash's stories appear to contain this warning nor do any of those I briefly recounted from the press, nor the story of the Edsel nor Project Intercept.

CHANGE

This is the third major point of agreement. Not only do many of the writers mention it—Ross and Kami, Simmonds, Smith, Houston, Cohen and Hartigan—but it comes out in the King case very clearly, where the market changed, and in the case of Cornes Tideswell where labour practices changed, but apparently the management did not restyle the company in response.

ACCOUNTING MANIPULATIONS

This is mentioned by Ross and Kami, Barmash, Deeson and *Business Week*. Failure seems often to be associated with fixing the books or fiddling the figures. Sometimes it is done with the aid of tame auditors, sometimes because of greed even to the point of fraud (particularly noted by Barmash, Deeson and Hartigan).

RAPID EXPANSION

Oddly enough, only Hartigan and Cohen mention overtrading. This is odd because rapid expansion was surely an element in the collapse of Stirling Homex, Piccadilly Estates, Wilstar and Mainline. Barmash, Brooks and Simmonds all draw attention to the big project that goes wrong—Freedomland, Edsel, Kariba, and so on.

ECONOMIC CYCLE

Equally odd is that only Hartigan mentions the economic cycle; but a cyclical depression (admittedly of very rare proportions) caused many of the construction and property company failures in 1974 as described in the Press. Again, no one mentioned inflation.

I am now reduced to listing items that only one or two authors mentioned and at that level of agreement I am not sure it is worth doing. Looking through the lists I can see no other items that recur again and again.

Hardly anyone mentions planning (except Ross and Kami) and none of Barmash's stories nor the press stories seem to hinge on its lack. Dolly girls are mentioned and flamboyance is certainly a common trait in Barmash, Deeson and Stirling Homex. Gearing is barely mentioned, although, while Barmash and Cohen say how easy it is to obtain capital, Hartigan says that shortage of capital is a severe cause of failure. Morale is mentioned, government action is, bad luck is, a sense of urgency is, prestige is, unwillingness to take advice is, greed is, public opinion is, labour troubles are. Of course, we must brace ourselves to the possibility that predicting failure is not just difficult, it is impossible—the Edsel failure was apparently quite unpredictable even with hindsight.

3. *What the experts say*

Although the glimmer of a coherent picture emerged eventually from the widely differing views of the writers in the last chapter, it was on the whole all rather disappointing. Two or three pieces in the puzzle did fit neatly together but a lot of them did not. In this chapter I shall record the views of several experts in failure whom I went to see during 1974 in an attempt to improve the consensus. By 'expert in failure' I do not mean someone who has failed repeatedly in business—they have a somewhat distorted view of the affair, as we saw from Brough in chapter 1. No, I mean insolvency managers, accountants, Receivers, bankers, investment analysts —that sort of expert. Most of the interviews I had with them lasted considerably less than an hour; they had to be brief because I wanted to see only those experts whose high reputation in their specialist field would guarantee a profound contribution to the subject and that meant going to see some very busy people. In the summaries that follow, some of the names are pseudonyms.

Cork

Mr Kenneth Cork is the senior partner of one of the largest firms of insolvency accountants in Britain and has, I imagine, as much experience in this field as anyone in the country.

One of the main causes of failure, he said, is simply bad communications; the boss does not know what is happening to the business as a whole. In large companies especially, great waves of paper deluge the chief executive with thousands of tiny disjointed facts. Only occasionally does one come across a system that tells the chief executive in simple form what he wants to know, which is how his business is doing as a whole.

When Mr Cork takes over a company in his role of Receiver he insists on the senior managers knowing half a dozen absolutely essential figures at all times. The figures differ slightly for each type of company but in general they include turnover, rate of gross profit, creditors, overdraft and, most important, when the next peak demand for cash will occur and how it is to be met. Most senior managers have to learn that he expects them to know such things; Mr Cork not only expects them to know these figures but to update them continuously in their minds as new relevant information comes in.

Another major cause is failure to keep up with a change in technology. Mr Cork believes that if managers have their ear to the ground they should have plenty of warning of such changes even in these days. Well-run companies should not fail from this cause.

Mr Cork has a golden rule: never undertake a development the cost of which you cannot write off and still remain in existence. He quoted the case of Handley Page who tried to develop a new airliner called the Jetstream. The project was delayed for two years by technical and other difficulties and that was the end of Handley Page. Much the same occurred with Rolls-Royce and the RB 211, and with Lockheed and the TriStar. They all broke Cork's golden rule: they undertook a project that was so large in relation to their size that, when it went wrong (and projects often do, especially if you are banking on them going right) it brought down the whole company. Nor is this rule applicable only to technological projects; the same principle is involved when, for example, a parent company guarantees the loans of a subsidiary company on such a scale that if the subsidiary fails so would the parent. If you cannot meet an obligation, do not enter into it.

I asked if greed was a common cause of failure. Mr Cork was sure it was not. Companies are built up by people who want to succeed, who want to construct a large organization, who are determined to make their restaurant, say, better than anyone else's restaurant. It is achievement that motivates, not greed. If you aim to provide a service to the community and if you do it well then the money will roll in, but if you aim just to make money for itself, then people cease to trust you. I also asked who was likely to see the first symptoms of failure. Mr Cork replied that it was not the auditor's job to look for signs of failure so they would not see them even though they were quite well placed to do so. The first people to see the signs of failure would surely be the managers, although quite frequently they attempt to conceal these facts from themselves and the accounts. Their motive for doing this is very seldom evil and almost never fraudulent; it is done simply to keep going 'until better times come'.

One of the most satisfying trends in the job of Receiver over the past few decades has been the shift in emphasis from simply selling off the assets of a failed company and winding it up to the more constructive approach of trying to rescue as much of it as possible and seeing it live on as a going concern. The Receiver today is, and much prefers to be, a doctor; he is only an undertaker when the company has failed beyond recall.

Leach

Sir Ronald Leach is the senior partner of a very well-known international firm of accountants.

His opinion on one matter is definitive: if the management of a company is good then that company will only fail as a result of bad luck. One aspect of good management is to avoid overtrading—indeed he would like to go further and recommend every company to have something in reserve even though he knew that this was an old-fashioned ideal. But the plain fact is that far too many companies today are far too highly geared and are just asking for trouble. 'Whizz kids can whizz down as well as up', said Sir Ronald.

Another aspect of good management is to calculate one's cash flow position for months or even years ahead. Many companies do not yet include a Source and Application of Funds Table in their annual accounts and they therefore possibly do not even know what their cash flow position was for the past year, let alone for the coming one. Not to know this is just plain bad management.

He also thought that top managers should be the first to see the symptoms of failure. It would not normally be the auditors, nor the stock market, nor necessarily outside directors. Investment analysts might see the signs. Bank managers, Sir Ronald thought, might, because some of them have a highly developed nose for trouble and can judge their clients accurately. But even if they do detect the early symptoms that does not help very much, because a bank only needs to do something when it feels its loans are threatened, and this may be long after most of the equity value of the company has been lost. There is another reason: if a bank has lent money to a company the last thing it wants to do is to draw attention to that company's troubles.

So if the managers do not know they are running into trouble (or do know but do nothing about it) there is no one else around whose job is to warn them or keep them up to scratch. All sorts of people have tried to devise systems for supervising managers—Lord O'Brien, Lord Watkinson and Brandon Rhys Williams, MP, for example—but Sir Ronald does not really think any of them are fully effective. The main problem is that top managers find their style is cramped by such supervision and their risk-taking flair is impaired. But in any case how are we to staff these supervisory positions? The number of intelligent, independent, incorruptible citizens we would need is far beyond the supply.

No, it looks as though we must continue to rely on the managers. But they must watch their cash flow and their gearing especially when inflation is at a high rate. The auditors should stick to their role which is to draw attention to irregularities and to express an opinion on the annual accounts; as for fraud, Sir Ronald believes it is very rare indeed.

Paterson

Some of Mr Paterson's views are almost diametrically opposite those of Mr Cork and Sir Ronald. He says that auditors *do* see the symptoms of failure before the managers do and that fraud, or misfeasance, is extremely common. One might conclude that these two opinions were irreconcilable but I believe that the answer to this paradox is quite simple; Mr Cork's and Sir Ronald's clients are nearly all large companies often managed by highly trained professionals while Mr Paterson, who is the senior partner of a firm of accountants, in a county town, deals mainly with companies that are, by comparison, minuscule. Some of them are just one man and his wife or brother, some are family businesses employing a few other employees. Very few employ as many as, say, 50 people.

Mr Paterson, then, believes he often sees the signs before the proprietors do—sometimes as much as two or even three years before failure. Typical danger signs are high turnover and low assets indicating that the company may be overtrading. He believes—and here Mr Burgess, the firm's insolvency manager, strongly agreed—that he could save half the firms that eventually fail if he was invited to help them in these early stages. But, almost invariably, managers refuse to face the facts and will not accept help until it is too late.

Mr Paterson identifies several causes of failure. One of these is that many of his clients do not use any form of budgetary control and a few of them keep no records of any sort. While they may feel they know how the business is doing, in fact they do not. Another problem is the valuation of assets and work in progress. For a small builder, for example, work in progress may represent an enormous proportion of the total value of his business. But how do you value 10 bungalows in varying states of construction? The tax inspector insists on a value that may be quite reasonable from his point of view but which is totally unrealistic if the proprietor is forced to sell one of these half-built bungalows in the market because he urgently needs the cash.

Mr Paterson also feels that banks are often not blameless; they have tended in the past to make it too easy to obtain loans—sometimes even when the business is obviously failing. He particularly feels that there is, on occasion, a lack of communication between the banks and company directors to the extent that sufficient discussion does not take place until the value of the company has fallen to the point at which their loan is at risk, and by then the company is probably lost beyond recall. The result, of course, is that when the crash comes it is worse than it might otherwise have been.

This last point is interesting because Mr Paterson believes that many of the managers who know their company is failing do their best to conceal the fact even from themselves. A typical remark is 'we only need another contract like the one from Ghana . . .'. Meanwhile, although the position may be hopeless, the bank loans keep them going.

In nearly half the cases of failure that Mr Paterson sees, he suspects that there has been some form of misfeasance. He is not saying that fraud is a major cause of failure; he is saying that some proprietors or directors do misuse their position. A typical ploy is to start a business leaving its main asset, a building, say, or some land, in the proprietor's own name and then milk the company for salary and expenses. He believes that the laws of limited liability are too lax and too easily allow people who have no intention of ever paying their creditors to form limited companies—sometimes repeatedly.

Thorn

Mr C. A. Thorn specializes in insolvency for one of the big international firms of accountants.

He believes that a potent cause of failure is biting off more than one can chew and he quotes the case of a company run by two technologists who incurred research costs far beyond the capacity of their company to sustain. Indeed, they seemed to be wholly ignorant of finance, had no idea what their product cost, had no budgetary control (although the firm employed a thousand people), but, by some miracle, had borrowed several million pounds from the banks, compared with £100 000 of their own equity.

Mr Thorn believes that 99 per cent of failures are due to bad management, the other one per cent to bad luck. And a huge slice of those due to bad management are really due to bad communications—the information system either does not exist at all or is not giving the senior managers what they need. For example, most managers know the turnover figures for their firm, often in some detail, but this is almost useless unless they also know what the profits are. Mr Thorn sets great store by contribution analysis; it is one of the major tools in the prevention of failure, for it shows the company which of its activities are making a profit and which a loss. But that alone is not enough. Firms must also have a budgetary control system although Mr Thorn estimates that as many as half the firms in the country do not have one.

He identified two causes of failure. One is high gearing, and the recent trend towards ever-higher gearing would seem to foreshadow more failures. The other is when the firm's managers neglect to read the signs of change in the firm's technology or its market or in the economy. One symptom of impending trouble is the appearance of imbalance; for example, if research expenditure rises faster than turnover or creditors rise faster than debtors.

Mr Thorn laid particular emphasis on the role of the Receiver. In the old days a Receiver simply came in, took over, sold up and distributed the cash to the creditors. Now a Receiver's aim is to cure the patient rather than to dismember him. Unfortunately a good deal of surgery is often required and it is nearly always necessary to dismiss some employees and sell some assets before the profitable core of the business has been exposed. There nearly always is a profitable core. The result of the Receiver's surgery is a smaller going concern that is worth a good deal more to the creditors than a list of assets for sale. And, of course, although no surgery is painless, at least some of the employees still have their jobs.

Harvey

Another very well-known figure in the insolvency world is A. H. Harvey. When he is called in as Receiver he can see a great many symptoms of failure but, of course, by then it is too late. A lot of people who know the company would have seen a lot of symptoms for months or years past but may not have recognized them as symptoms of failure at the time. Thus the customers would have noticed the firm pressing them to pay their invoices; suppliers would have noticed the firm delaying payment to them; employees would have noticed the lower pay packets and the dingy offices and the delay in maintaining plant and the postponed capital expenditure authorizations. Many middle managers would have noticed these things; the chief buyer would have and the credit controller and the bought ledger clerks. So would the bank clerks who would perhaps have seen the firm's cashier rushing round to the bank to pay in a cheque so the wages could be paid. All sorts of measures, more or less desperate, would have been seen for months before failure.

So, says Mr Harvey, there are plenty of symptoms, the trouble is to recognize them as such at the time. But even if the managers do recognize them, many managers do not take emergency action, do not call in experts, do not cut back, because they hope 'the clouds will roll away'. This is a great pity because large parts of the firm could be saved if they called in a Receiver or a consultant earlier; even after failure something can usually be saved. Indeed, it is the Receiver's job to find the profitable kernel and pare down to it.

What about causes? Mr Harvey mentioned three. One is overtrading—the company expands too fast and runs out of cash. This is very common. Another is that the managers lose control because the company's affairs become too complex for the information system to cope with. Another is simply that the company should never have been started in the first place! Mr Harvey had seen a number of these cases of which the most outrageous was a firm which built a completely new factory for its completely new product, a marvel of modern science. Unfortunately the product did not sell and the firm failed having never made a penny profit. It seems, says Mr Harvey, that firms run by engineers (and occasionally by marketing men) are particularly prone to such ignominy.

Allen

R. S. Allen is a leading member of the Society of Investment Analysts and a director of a well-known firm of London stockbrokers.

It had been clear for some years before the failure that something was sadly wrong at Rolls-Royce, he told me. One did not have to be an accountant to see that the return on capital, the profit margin, the treatment of research as an asset, and so on, were symptomatic of a long-standing malaise. His firm had ensured that their clients did not hold shares in Rolls-Royce; nor was Rolls-Royce the only example of a company that was clearly in trouble. He named three companies which were then (August 1974) on his black list, of which two, Alfred Herbert and British Leyland, have since asked for financial assistance from the government.

Thus it is certainly possible in some cases to be fairly confident of diagnosing trouble from even a cursory study of the published accounts and a more detailed study might uncover less blatant cases. But the comparatively recent appearance of inflation at high rates was bound to make such analysis much more difficult to do, not only for the outsider, but also for the manager. Profit is calculated by subtracting one huge figure from another huge figure; the errors inherent in this calculation have always been considerable but now, due to inflation, they are enormous. The valuation of stocks, of work in progress, of property, all are now infinitely more difficult. Profit is a fragile thing. It always has been, but now inflation must be counted as a major potential cause of failure because companies will simply not know whether they are making a profit or a loss. Not only will it be more difficult for the managers to know this, it will also be more difficult for the outsider to know how the company is doing.

There is another implication, too. Inflation will make life even easier for managers who wish to deceive the observer. Mr Allen has seen several cases of deceit and of downright fraud. The most common device is to inflate the value of the company with the passive, or occasionally active, support of the auditors. He particularly remembers one case of a proprietor of a building firm, a big, hearty showman, whose firm became the largest client of the accountants who audited his books. Not wishing to lose such an important customer the auditor allowed the firm to value all its completed houses at full market price. Mr Allen believes he has seen enough of this sort of thing to say that fraud is a significant cause of failure.

Although the inherent inaccuracies of accounting practice, not to mention inflation and deceit, make observation difficult, there is one tool that the trained observer can still use with as much confidence as ever. This is the company visit. It is surprising how much 'feel' one develops after a few such visits. On one occasion Mr Allen visited a provincial company with a party of other analysts from London. On completing the visit they returned to the near-by railway station from which several of them telephoned immediate 'sell' instructions to their brokers! On another occasion Mr Allen lunched with the three senior directors of a public company making a well-known scientific device. One of them was slightly inebriated, another was unbearably conceited and the third was a smooth-talking salesman. It was, felt Mr Allen, no coincidence that their firm had recently not achieved its profit forecast. He advised 'sell' and soon after the firm failed.

I have recounted these stories, which at first glance appear to be mere gossip, because Mr Allen's precept 'Go there' is an important one, and because companies are run by directors and directors are human beings; what sort of people they are has a highly significant impact on the company. One might go so far as to say that the nature of the top management team in a company is of greater significance for success or failure than any of the company's products or skills or physical assets.

Curtis

Mr Leonard Curtis practises in the West End of London away from the City where many other accountancy and insolvency firms are to be found. His firm is smaller than Mr Cork's but larger than Mr Paterson's and I wondered if his views were in some sense midway between these two thus reflecting the average size of company that their firms normally deal with. In respect of fraud his views do seem to come midway, for Mr Curtis estimates that less than one failure in a hundred (but possibly more than one in two hundred) is accompanied by dishonesty or deceit or misfeasance. But his views on dishonesty were interesting in another sense also.

From the moment when a man starts a business he makes dozens of decisions a day, some of them very difficult. But the biggest decision he will ever make is the decision to wind up. He has to admit failure, he has to acknowledge, in public, that he has wasted almost his entire working life. It is by far his most difficult decision. So he does what most of us would do, he postpones it. Sometimes he puts it off for years, long after he should have stopped. Is this dishonest? Or is it normal business optimism—'After all', he says to himself, 'we only need another order like we had last Christmas.' By the time he admits defeat the air is thick with writs. 'Reality', said Mr Curtis, 'is where optimism meets pessimism. I would not like to say that a man was dishonest for not recognizing where this point was.'

One main cause of failure is the common fault of not taking account of the ups and downs of business. Many companies are heavily dependent upon everything going right. Suddenly it does not; a customer takes his business elsewhere, a big project fails or whatever. Too much dependence on something that may let you down has always been a common cause, but is even more common today when most companies run on high gearing. And it should be remembered that while managers are going for growth and higher turnover, which they find exhilarating, their bankers find it rather frightening. They may be so alarmed at what they call 'overtrading' that they may try to get their loan back while it is still covered by asset values.

As for symptoms, Mr Curtis thought there was no lack of them and many were visible to outsiders. Customers might see the company cutting prices to improve flagging sales, suppliers would notice the company was taking longer to pay. Perhaps a new product fails to sell. Possibly the stock market would see something (but it must be noted that even in Britain there are few quoted companies relative to the total) and possibly the auditors. But it is the managers who will be first to know and either they do something to stop the rot or they do not. If they do not then others will start to notice.

There is one vital tool that managers must use—the cash flow forecast.

A forecast of cash flow for a few months ahead is probably inadequate: one for a year or two is sensible for most companies. Many companies now do such forecasts but then put the figures away in a drawer and forget them. This is absurd, of course; the forecast must be updated. If it is not updated it is useless; if it is, it is invaluable.

Scarlett

G. W. Scarlett is the general manager of Britain's largest industrial finance company providing finance for small and medium-sized businesses. At the top of his list of the causes of failure Mr Scarlett puts overtrading. It is true that most successful companies overtrade at some time or another and so it can be done without endangering the firm—but only if management know what they are doing and keep it under control. A second major cause is that of being left behind by changes in technology. Normally this was quite inexcusable because any management that was even half alive should be aware of all the technical changes that are going on in relevant fields and, given normal loyalty that many customers extend to their suppliers, there is usually plenty of time in which these technological changes can be made.

There were other causes of failure: quarrels in family businesses could be very serious. So could some of the personality traits of some of the technologists who found their own businesses for, when these expand beyond a certain point, they cannot cope with the financial or the human aspects of business. Another cause is the mistiming of capital expenditure. It can happen that a company, encouraged by rising demand, decides to build a factory which, because of the time-lags today, is completed just when the economy turns down. Mr Scarlett thought that fraud was a very minor cause indeed—his firm might have seen ten cases of fraud in the 3000 companies they had dealt with in the past few decades.

Turning to symptoms of troubles ahead, Mr Scarlett thought that top managers should see them first. If they do not, then this itself suggests they are not competent and it is reasonable to guess that matters will deteriorate until others start to see the signs. Auditors might see them, but it was not their job to look for them. Bankers are not normally in a position to see them. Middle management quite often does see them—after all, the symptoms of failure are often observable for some years before the failure actually occurs. Middle management will know that the product is outdated, that stocks are rising, that certain decisions have been postponed, that customers are complaining, that repairs have not been carried out, that cash is short, and so on.

As to the value of non-executive directors, Mr Scarlett agreed that quite often they will not see the signs of future failure because they are not being fed with adequate information on which to form a judgement. It is essential that non-executive directors have the confidence of management and a close and harmonious relationship therewith. If this is achieved they have more chance of spotting and foreseeing future troubles.

As to prevention: Mr Scarlett believes that the keys to good management include corporate planning, careful scrutiny of cash flow statements which must be updated constantly and a proper system of authorizing capital expenditure (which must always be fully justified on basis of profit return).

Dunscombe

P. D. Dunscombe is a very experienced accountant and senior partner of a well-known international firm of accountants.

He told me that 1974 marked a change in the business world of quite exceptional proportions. Suddenly that year the decades of growth to which we have all become accustomed came to a halt in very many sectors of activity all over the world. The result is that innumerable companies, having geared up their equity for continued expansion, are finding it difficult to earn enough profit to cover their loan commitments adequately. Now this means that, almost over night, the key to running a business has become the management of cash flows.

Although the present circumstances are indeed exceptional, high gearing has always been a potent cause of failure. High gearing coupled with the downswing of an economic cycle is the classic cause. But to these causes we must now add two new modern ones; the first is lack of flexibility in management decision-making, resulting from restrictions imposed by labour unions. Not to be able to modernize methods, not to be able to close down uneconomic activities—these are becoming severe handicaps. The other is interference by government in business decisions. Not to be able to raise prices when costs are rising is clearly as swift a way to failure as can be devised.

As to symptoms, Mr Dunscombe thought that occasionally an inspired pundit could forecast failure but that this was rare. Bankers should see the signs, especially as they were now bringing managers to account more frequently. Unfortunately, inflation generates such a smoke screen over most accounting information that it is becoming difficult for many people to read the danger signals. However, of all people, it should be the managers who first see trouble coming, although it is true that some managers —and especially some entrepreneurs—may try to hide the truth even from themselves. In view of this, it is always a useful safeguard to ensure that the finance function of a company is well represented on the board. Very often, and this is still particularly true in Britain, the board is dominated by technical men who may not so readily appreciate the firm's financial state unless a strong finance man can explain the situation in a stark and simple manner.

But perhaps the best safeguard of all, thought Mr Dunscombe, is for the firm to have a strong chairman. Many people do not understand the distinction between chairman and chief executive; the latter is the most senior manager who is judged, as all managers are, by results. But who should judge him? The answer is the chairman. It is his job to see that the chief executive is doing his job. Firms who combine the role of chairman with that of chief executive can seriously misunderstand the nature of business organization.

It was at this stage in my inquiries, having discussed failure with ten of the leading experts in the country, that I thought I could begin to see a pattern emerging. Indeed, although each expert had shone new light on the subject, I felt that an overall consensus had now been formed and that further interviews would yield only further detail rather than some major new principle. There was only one area of uncertainty in my mind. I understood that almost all companies were run by honest men and that their annual accounts were drawn up honestly. I also understood that only when a company was in difficulties would the proprietors or top managers deliberately begin to distort the accounts as a smokescreen. What I was not clear about, and where there still seemed to be conflicting views, was the extent of fraud. I therefore went to Scotland Yard for enlightenment.

Stockwell

Detective Superintendent Stockwell, one of the Heads of the Metropolitan

& City of London Company Fraud Department, and his collator, Sergeant Dennis, told me that they deal with over 300 cases a year in London. If you take the country as a whole the figure is probably 600 a year. The majority of these cases concern companies that are formed *deliberately as a fraud*—it does not include cases of fraud by individual employees of companies. (There are some 25 000 cases of fraud in the Metropolitan Police area each year, but these include a large number which have nothing at all to do with companies, such as passing dud cheques and so on.)

Superintendent Stockwell does confirm one impression I had gathered from the experts; there is a strong inverse correlation between fraud and size of company. It is rare that a fraud is committed by a company with more than 50 employees and most have only a dozen or less. So, for Britain at least, the impression given by some of the writers is a gross exaggeration. Fraud is an almost insignificant cause of failure. But that still leaves us with several hundred firms a year that are specifically formed for fraud.

A typical example is the Long Firm fraud, in which Mr A and Mr B form a company and recruit, say, six salesmen. They comb through the residential areas of Southtown selling central heating systems at £300. From each householder they obtain £30 advance payment and, without realizing it, the householder also signs a 'satisfaction note'. This note enables AB and Co. to obtain enough finance from a hire purchase company to order £300 worth of copper pipe and other materials, which is promptly sold through a previously arranged outlet. AB and Co. can keep this up until the citizens of Southtown, no longer satisfied by A and B's explanations of delay, complain to the authorities. A and B then disappear. Later they reappear in Northtown as the XY Folding Attic Ladder Company. Or they might try the 'Spanish land fraud' or perhaps the 'trade directories fraud'.

Of course, one is not permitted to become a director of a company in Britain while one is an undischarged bankrupt, but one can become a director even if one has a conviction for fraud! Indeed there are estimated to be 20 000 company directors in Britain with criminal records of some sort.

Superintendent Stockwell thought that it would not be so easy to defraud a well-managed company. Most good managers know their staff well enough to observe whether their life-style is consistent with their known financial circumstances. Most good bosses would also be a little suspicious of an employee who never went on holiday, was always first to arrive and last to leave the office, and never let anyone help him with his books. Nor should it be easy for even one of the new international gangs to defraud a well-managed company for long, for if the managers did not find them out the auditors would. The new international gangs of fraudsmen, unlike the oldfashioned ones, are non-violent and, operating internationally on a scale much too large and complex for their rather small host nations to deal with, work behind the front of respectability.

They did not say so in so many words, but I felt that both Superintendent Stockwell and Sergeant Dennis were worried by a shift in public opinion. A few decades ago it was considered immoral to live on credit; now, of course, hire purchase and overdrafts are universally accepted. But a new movement of opinion seems to be in progress concerning fraud; it is still considered grossly immoral to defraud an individual person, of course—public attitudes are firm on that—but to defraud a company, well that is somehow different. And a big company, well, that is very different.

Addenda

At this point I would like to add three further pieces of the jigsaw. The first relates to the remarks by several experts concerning the rising level of gearing in recent years. The figures for British industry show that in the late sixties profits retained by companies for reinvestment totalled some £3bn and bank lending to companies totalled £0·5bn. By the early seventies retained profits had doubled to £6bn, but bank lending had multiplied eightfold to £4bn (bn is billion, of course). These figures cannot be used to calculate gearing but they do bring out very clearly that gearing has increased enormously.

The second piece concerns auditors. Several experts and writers have noted how difficult it is for auditors to know whether a figure given to them by a proprietor should be accepted or not. One has to bear in mind that an auditor will not qualify his report unless he feels on very strong ground, for it is a serious step to take. It is interesting in this context to read Paragraph 323 of the interim report of the Department of Trade and Industry on International Learning Systems Corporation Limited. This describes first how the firm's draft accounts for 1967/8 showed a profit of £806 000. After being audited this figure became £40 000. But there was some doubt about even this and when a second firm of auditors was asked their opinion, the figure became a *loss* of £2 589 000. Although such a wide spread of opinion is very rare it does show how flexible are the rules of accountancy, even in Britain where accountancy methods have led the world. And this example comes from an era when inflation did not exceed five per cent per annum, so the inflation smokescreen was not yet in operation.

My third addendum concerns the scathing remarks some experts made on the usefulness of outside directors. In my own experience not all of these watchdogs are comatose, but a case where one was occurred recently. I was asked to join a board meeting of a company to discuss with the directors how corporate planning could best be introduced. One of the part-time directors present represented a well-known bank which had recently made considerable loan to the company. His job was to ensure that this loan was not in jeopardy and he had been on the board for some six months. When I asked to be shown round the factory this director asked if he could come too. It became plain on our way round that he had not been inside the factory before and he was clearly shocked by the state of dilapidation that confronted him.

Interim conclusions

Most of the experts whose views I have collected together in this chapter are accountants by profession, while most of the writers were journalists or managers. One would not expect a summary of conclusions from this chapter to contain the same items as from the last one. Nor does it. Although there is some emphasis on bad management there is less analysis on precisely what aspects of bad management lead to failure. On the other hand, there is a wealth of analytical opinion on the financial aspects of failure.

MANAGEMENT

That failure is caused by bad management was specifically mentioned by Leach, Thorn, Allen, Scarlett and Dunscombe but it was implicit in all the experts' contributions. The only management fault that was precisely identified was the failure to allow a strong enough financial opinion to be heard at top levels, although some of the unusual personality traits of top managers were also mentioned by Scarlett.

ACCOUNTANCY INFORMATION

This emerged as a major potential element in failure. There seem to be four main deficiencies that occur frequently in failed companies. They have no cash flow forecasts (Cork, Leach, Curtis, Scarlett and Dunscombe specifically mentioned these). They have no costing system (Thorn and Scarlett). They have no system of budgetary control (Cork, Paterson and Thorn), and there is the problem of valuing assets (Paterson and Allen).

MANAGERS SEE THE SYMPTOMS FIRST

Many experts suggest that some symptoms can be seen as much as several years before failure occurs. Apart from Paterson, all the experts believe that managers are first to see trouble ahead unless they are so bad that it is really past belief. With the possible exception of very small firms, then, auditors do not often know before the managers, nor do bankers, nor the stock market, nor do outside directors who, by all accounts, are in a permanent coma. It is not the auditor's job, however, to act as watchdog in this way, although it is the job of some outside directors and the stock market. The banks are not interested unless their loans are threatened.

As for other observers, a number of them are well placed to see certain symptoms—customers, suppliers and, in particular, middle managers—but these symptoms are often of a non-financial character including, for example, quality, delivery delays, poor maintenance and so on. Other observers, journalists, investment analysts and others may be able to see the signs in the company's published accounts. A visit to the company to meet its directors and see its facilities is most useful (Allen and Scarlett).

CREATIVE ACCOUNTING

A phenomenon that frequently appears associated with failure is 'creative accounting'. The explanation (Cork, Paterson, Allen, Curtis and Dunscombe) is that although the managers know perfectly well that the company is in trouble they refuse to admit it and start putting up a smoke-screen—which usually takes the form of publishing the accounts in the most optimistic colours possible. Sometimes this optimism crosses the line into dishonest or illegal or downright fraudulent statements, but this is rare except among small companies. (The figures we have for fraud are that 600 a year are deliberate; as many as half the small companies that fail are involved in misfeasance if not fraud; so are between one in 100 to one in 300 medium-sized firms (Curtis and Scarlett); but large firms hardly ever are.) Creative accounting, then, is most often a defence mechanism, and this refusal to admit failure is possibly part of the normal businessman's psychological equipment which also accounts for his refusal to accept advice and for such statements as, 'the clouds will roll away', 'until better times come', 'we only need another order like the one from Ghana', and '. . . like the order we had last Christmas' (quoted by Harvey, Cork, Paterson and Curtis, respectively). Since, for tax reasons, most companies try not to overstate their profits any firm that does try to must be suspect.

Accountancy is a somewhat flexible set of rules made even more flexible by inflation. Auditors can be persuaded not to notice some special pieces of flexibility but this seems to be an exceedingly rare occurrence.

OVERTRADING

Leach, Paterson, Harvey, Curtis and Scarlett point to overtrading as a major cause of failure. By this they mean that the company's sales, stock levels and general scale of activity increases faster than their capital. The result is a shortage of cash which can lead to insolvency. But, as Scarlett said, many firms overtrade at times and get away with it because they know they are doing it and keep it under control.

BANKS AND GEARING

There was wide agreement that many companies in 1974 were far too highly geared. This was especially dangerous because there were signs that in 1975 the world economy could be further depressed and high gearing plus an economic downturn is the classic causal nutcracker (Leach, Thorn, Curtis and Dunscombe). Curtis particularly notes that in addition to being vulnerable to an economic downturn, a highly geared company is vulnerable to any of the other myriad ups and downs of business. Paterson believes that high gearing is at least partly due to generosity on the part of some banks.

THE BIG PROJECT

Thorn and Cork draw attention to the proclivity of companies to undertake projects that are beyond their resources. When these fail, so do the companies unless they adopt Cork's rule: do not enter into an obligation if you cannot meet it.

CHANGE

Cork, Thorn and Scarlett believe that companies often fail because they do not move with the changing world, particularly changes in technology. In most cases such a failure is rank bad management for, even today, there is usually plenty of time.

RESCUE

There seemed to be wide agreement (Cork, Paterson, Thorn and Harvey) that even after a company has called in the Receiver there is often a profitable core still left. This could be rescued from the wreckage. The earlier the Receiver, or some other company doctor, could be called in the more could be rescued. Unfortunately, accepting advice on how to run his business is not a notable feature of the businessman's personality and he waits until the last moment.

MISCELLANEOUS VIEWS

Dunscombe draws particular attention to the distinction between the job of the chairman and that of the chief executive. He also notes two new causes of failure; restrictions and restraints imposed by organized labour and by governments. Leach notes that a number of methods of supervising top managers have been devised but without much success; in any case there is the problem of finding suitable staff. Stockwell and Paterson are irritated by the ease with which a company director can perpetrate his frauds time after time under present legislation. There seems general agreement that bad luck is a rare cause of failure. Harvey recalls several companies that failed because they should never have been started.

It is a strange fact that some of these minority views turn out later on to have an importance far beyond the minor place they have had to be given here.

4. *What Professor Altman says*

As I have said before, most of the books on failure, which all seem to be called *Great Business Crashes*, are written by journalists. Most of them are concerned more with telling a story, often the personal story of the central figure in the disaster, than with cold analysis, but we have seen in chapter 2 that this approach, in addition to being mildly entertaining, reveals some important general lessons which I want to discuss further at the end of the book when all the pieces of our puzzle have been laid out ready to be fitted together.

Now I want to turn to the other end of the scale from the journalists, to a noted academic, one of the very few who works in this field: Edward I. Altman. He graduated at the University of California, Los Angeles, in 1967 and has since been particularly interested in bankruptcy. He was Visiting Professor at the Centre d'Enseignment Superieur des Affaires and was an adviser to the Presidential-Congressional Commission on the National Bankruptcy Laws of the USA. At present he is Associate Professor of Finance at New York University.

So far as I know, his book, *Corporate Bankruptcy in America*, is the only serious work on this subject. When I say 'serious' I mean analytical, of course; I do not mean that other books, such as those of the journalists, are not worthy of serious attention. Failure is a very human event; journalists certainly can see aspects of it that evade Altman's equations.

Altman starts his book as I start mine—with an expression of surprise that although failure, collapse and bankruptcy are facts of corporate life and always have been, yet there is a striking lack of any integrated framework for the subject. What he wants to do, he says, is to employ modern techniques, such as multivariate statistical analysis, to look at the linkage between failure and say, economic trends, and to develop some means of predicting failure. But first he starts with some facts and figures. These all relate to the USA, of course.

Facts and figures for the USA

Altman distinguishes between failure, insolvency and bankruptcy. *Failure* is merely when the company does not earn an adequate return on risk capital and it can go on doing this for years without closing down; somehow or other it goes on being able to pay its bills. It is worth noting, in passing, that according to Dun and Bradstreet's figures quoted by Altman, less than 0·4 per cent of companies that discontinue every year do so because of 'failure'. Thus in the mid sixties nearly 400 000 businesses closed down each year but only 15 000 of them actually failed. And also in passing, 445 000 new businesses were launched into the pool of over 4½ million going concerns. So, out of all the firms operating in an average year, nearly 10 per cent will be new ones less than a year old, about 9 per cent will close down during the year and 0·4 per cent will actually fail. Two things about these figures are surprising. The very high rate of turnover—9 or 10 per cent of all businesses come or go during the year; and the very low rate of failure—only about one business in 250 fails, apparently. However, it is nowhere stated why all those other companies go out of business each year; and these amount to about one business in 11!

Insolvency is a much more definitive word than failure; it means you cannot pay your bills when they fall due. This can be a purely temporary situation; it is then a *technical insolvency*. But 'insolvency in a bankruptcy sense' is much more serious. It implies that the firm's liabilities exceed a fair valuation of its assets; the company has a negative net worth. Oddly enough, as Altman remarks, you know when you are technically insolvent because of the unmistakeable fact that you have no cash with which to pay your bills, but you may not know that you have hit the far more serious version of insolvency because it is so difficult to value assets unless they are actually sold off and a true market value thus placed upon them.

Bankruptcy is often used synonymously with insolvency, i.e., when there is a negative net worth. In another sense it refers to the actual declaration of bankruptcy together with a petition by a company to a court to liquidate its assets or to attempt a recovery programme of some sort and it is then called a *bankruptcy-reorganization*. This reorganization is designed to keep at least part of the firm going if it is thought to be worth more to its creditors as a going concern than as a dead one. Altman then describes the US bankruptcy laws, which differ from those in Europe especially in the case of railroad bankruptcies (see p. 111).

The last stage for a bankrupt company, assuming reorganization is not successful, is *liquidation*. Here all the company's assets are sold off and all its creditors paid in a strictly laid down sequence; it is rare in an involuntary liquidation (i.e., one requested by creditors) for all creditors to be paid in full. In a voluntary liquidation (normally called for by the shareholders) payment in full is usual.

Altman notes that the failure rate has not increased in the past few decades—i.e., the number of failures per 10 000 existing firms has not increased. But the failure liability *has* increased—i.e., the dollar liabilities per bankrupt firm has increased in line with inflation and the growing size of companies. In 1970, for example, no less than 279 million-dollar firms went bust. His figures for the age of firms going bankrupt are almost identical to those of Brough (p. 7). Brough says that of all failures, about a quarter are two years old or less, 60 per cent are five years or less and only 21 per cent are more than 10 years old. Altman's figures (based on Dun and Bradstreet) are: one-third are less than three years old, 53 per cent less than five and 23 per cent over 10 years. Altman further notes the stability of some of these figures over long periods of time: except for a period soon after the war, the percentage of less-than-five-year-olds was never more than 58·9 per cent or less than 53·0 per cent of total failures. Out of all the failures that occur on both sides of the Atlantic, then, well over half are companies that are less than five years old. This has been so for many years. And, perhaps surprisingly in view of that figure, only 2 per cent of failures are firms less than one year old.

Altman briefly reviews previous works on the causes of failure. The main conclusion of these studies is that there is a wide variety of causes. He says that most of these studies conclude that failure is preventable, but Altman believes that mere causal analysis cannot provide a sound basis for prevention. He believes that prevention can best come by detecting the impending crisis far enough ahead to do something. His scepticism as to the value of merely enumerating possible causes is underlined by the fact that you get completely different explanations of failure depending upon who you ask—the managers or the creditors (or the Receivers—see Brough again, p. 7). Altman quotes a 1932 study which showed that 'inefficient management' was cited as a cause three times more often by creditors than by the owners of the failed companies. For what they are worth, Department of Commerce statistics in 1932 showed that inefficient management, unwise use and extension of credit, adverse domestic and personal factors, and dishonesty and fraud were major causes. Dewing has listed: competition, unprofitable expansion, cessation of public demand, excess payment of capital charges. Dun and Bradstreet show that 90 per cent of failures in 1969 were due to poor management in one form or another (in the creditor's view) thus: lack of, or unbalanced, experience—41·5 per cent; incompetence 45·6 per cent; neglect 2·8 per cent; fraud 1·2 per cent; disaster 1·4 per cent and unknown 7·1 per cent. (In the previous chapter Thorn said one per cent of failures were due to 'bad luck'. These figures suggest it is 1·4 per cent!)

External factors

Common sense would suggest that when economic activity levels off or declines, the number of company failures would increase, and vice versa. And so it is. But Altman wished to examine this association more closely and to learn what other factors outside the firm itself mainly affect failures. He developed a number of equations in order to examine the influence on failure rates of money market conditions, investor expectations and so on. It is generally believed, for example, that a credit squeeze is one of the most potent causes of collapse—many of the experts and writers I have described here mention this.

Altman believes that a credit squeeze works like this. During periods of tight money (usually brought about by the government trying to damp down an over-active economy) credit will be rationed out to those who are thought to be the best risks. These are not likely to be small firms or those which are believed to be in trouble already, of course, but the larger, stronger companies. Not only that, but because the large firm often continues to invest even in times of high interest rates the proportion of loans going to the big firms must be much higher when money is tight than when it is abundant. These two influences, tight money and an anti-small, anti-marginal firm lending policy, naturally tend to precipitate a rise in the number of failures since the great majority of failures are small firms.

Investor expectations may also influence failure. When a nation's economy is expected to turn down, two things often happen; the failure rate rises and share prices fall due to investors losing confidence. It can happen that investors so lack confidence in a company that its shares are marked down to the point where creditors start pressing their claims and bring about the collapse of the company.

However, it is one thing to discuss these influences in general terms and quite another to show their links with failure rigorously and mathematically. This Altman does. It is not easy because the three factors we are discussing—economic cycles, credit availability and investor confidence—are all intimately interlinked (the statisticians call this multicollinearity). Not only that, but you have to find reliable measures for all these things—do you use GNP statistics to indicate economic activity or do you use corporate profit figures? How do you measure 'credit squeeze'? Just to show how intimately linked all these things are, consider the way in which the various influences we are discussing follow each other in a sequence during an economic cycle. Suppose in January the government cuts the supply of money and credit, then in March there will be an increase in failure liabilities, in April a downturn in the formation of new businesses, in May profits will begin to fall, in July the Stock Market Index will turn down and in September the GNP figures will fall. That, says Altman, is a typical sequence of indicators in a typical cycle (based on work by the National Bureau covering US business cycles from 1900–70).

Well, what are the results of his calculations? First, a firm's propensity to fail *is* greater during periods of reduced economic growth, poor stock market performance and, especially important, tight money supply. The failure rate (i.e., the number of failures per 10 000 businesses) does change before the GNP changes, although only by a few months perhaps (which suggests that failure rates might be a useful indicator of a turn in GNP). However, stock prices and money supply also change at about the same time as the failure rate changes and therefore these two are not very useful as leading indicators of failure rates. Looking at failure liabilities, however, the relationships are much less significant although there are signs that failure liabilities are linked to the number of firms in existence. And, oddly at first sight, money supply does not affect failure liabilities. The explanation is probably that the failure liabilities figure (i.e., the short-term liabilities of bankrupt companies) is dominated by the number of large bankruptcies, while credit changes affect mainly small ones, as suggested above.

Another slightly odd result is that the GNP figure seems to be more closely related to failure rates than the corporate profit figure—one would think this latter would be a much more direct and pertinent associate of failure than the rather more remote GNP indicator, and in fact many people use the trend in corporate profits as the most important failure predictor; Altman's statistical analysis shows that to do this is mistaken. One other negative conclusion from this study: one would think that, as the economic environment for companies became more hostile, bankers would demand a higher risk premium for lending to risky companies than to the blue chips. In other words, one would expect that Moody's Baa rate would rise further than the Aaa rate when the economic future looked poor. (Aaa ratings are given to the best quality company; Baa is a lower-to-medium quality company which lacks outstanding investment characteristics and has speculative characteristics as well.) But Altman could find no statistically significant relationship between the movement of these Moody rates and failure rate and one may possibly conclude that in difficult times banks prefer not to lend to the more risky companies at all rather than lend to them at higher rates of interest.

The equation linking failure rates with GNP, stock market index and money supply is:

$$\Delta FR = a_0 + a_1\,\Delta GNP_t + a_2\,\Delta SP_t + a_3 \Delta MS_t + e$$

where ΔFR is the change in the failure rate from one quarter of the year to the next, ΔGNP_t is the change in GNP (in $bn) between those quarters, ΔSP is the change in the Standard and Poor Index of Common Stock Prices, ΔMS is the change in the money supply in $bn and e is an error term. In this equation (there are several versions), Altman found that the constant term a_0 had a value of 1·54 for 1959–70, a_1 had a value of $-0{\cdot}122$, a_2 was $-0{\cdot}190$ and a_3 was $-0{\cdot}495$. Let us suppose, to give an example, that the GNP of the US falls by $5bn, that the Standard and

Poor Index falls by 10 points and that the government increases the money supply by $1bn. The equation becomes

$$\Delta FR = 1{\cdot}54 \quad -0{\cdot}122\times-5 \quad -0{\cdot}190\times-10-0{\cdot}495\times 1$$

$$= 1{\cdot}54+0{\cdot}610+1{\cdot}90-0{\cdot}495 \quad =3{\cdot}555$$

In other words, the failure rate would increase by nearly 3·6 and, assuming 4·5m businesses are in existence, 1620 more businesses would fail than if the above changes in GNP, etc., had not occurred between one quarter and the next. This equation may repay further study. One of its implications is that if there is no change in GNP, stock market or money supply from one given quarter to the next then nearly 700 more businesses will fail! (Because the constant $a_0 = 1{\cdot}54$ and there are 4·5 million businesses.) And a further implication is that, if the government expects GNP to fall by $1bn, the number of businesses that will fail will increase by 1·662 per 10 000 (other factors being constant) but this could be offset so that no extra businesses fail by increasing money supply by $3·36bn (assuming no change in the stock market). However, such games extend the equations well beyond the use for which they were designed. (And it would, of course, be necessary to recalculate these equations to establish the terms for each different national economy.)

Altman concludes this section on the influence of economic affairs on failure with two practical comments. First, if you run a company which is already faltering (low profits for some time, struggling to keep market shares, etc., etc.) and if it begins to look as though an economic downturn or credit squeeze may occur, then it might be very good sense to take drastic action at once. Seek a merger, perhaps, or even declare bankruptcy and reorganization under the National Bankruptcy Act (in the USA of course). If you do not do it now, you may find yourself in real trouble when the economy turns down. His second point is this: if you are looking for a way to predict failure, it is not enough just to look at the firm itself, at its management, accounting ratios, R&D effort and so on. All these are very important—see below—but never forget that there are powerful external forces acting from outside the firm as well, notably the three described above: GNP, money supply and stock market performance.

Internal factors

Obviously, however potent are the factors influencing failure that lie outside the firm, those within the firm must be paramount for otherwise all firms would fail whenever economic conditions turned sour! What these internal factors are must be considered next—but in a rather special way. Altman believes that traditional ratio analysis and interfirm comparison methods have lost some of their appeal and that newer techniques, such as multiple discriminant analysis (MDA), should be used to examine how these factors affect a company's propensity to fail.

The sort of ratio analysis that Altman is unhappy about are those that rely on just one or two individual ratios. It is perfectly possible to show that, say, a hundred companies that failed all had a return on capital of *x* or less. But this tends to lead to the conclusion that all companies with a return of less than *x* will fail. Obviously this is much too simple—what about liquidity, for example: surely even a company with a high return could fail if its liquidity ratio was poor? The answer is yes, of course. And the truth is that several ratios are of key significance. But if that is so, what weight do you give each ratio and how do you add them all up to yield a critical score below which a company will almost certainly fail and above which it almost certainly will not. Can we somehow add all these ratios together to give a single composite indicator of propensity to fail. Yes, says Altman, that is just what MDA does.

What Altman did to identify this indicator was to analyse the figures for 33 firms (with assets between \$0·7m and \$25·9m) which had filed bankruptcy petitions and for another 33 firms (paired sample on stratified random basis) which were 'non-bankrupt'. And, of course, the figures he studied all relate to the same years. He searched for significant differences in certain ratios between these two groups of companies, ratios such as those relating to liquidity, profits, gearing, and so on. Actually only five ratios turned out to be really important for bankruptcy prediction. The equation that gave the best results was this one:

$$Z = 0{\cdot}012X_1+0{\cdot}014X_2+0{\cdot}033X_3+0{\cdot}006X_4+0{\cdot}010X_5$$

The five ratios are as follows:

X_1 is working capital/total assets. To calculate $0{\cdot}012X_1$ then, you simply take the difference between current assets and current liabilities, divide by the total book value of the company and multiply by 0·012. That is the first term in the equation. It is worth noting that Altman did test two other liquidity ratios (the 'current' ratio and the 'quick' ratio) but working capital/total assets proved better. (He did not try, for technical reasons, the well known ratio: cash flow/debt.)

But now we have a major complication. The definition of total assets (also known as net assets, or capital employed) used in Britain is not the same as the US definition. In Britain, total assets is defined as current assets less current liabilities plus fixed assets (including investments, goodwill and so on). So for ICI in 1973, for example, total assets amounted to £2143m made up of current assets of £1330m, less current liabilities of £631m, plus fixed and others of £1444m. But if ICI was an American company, its total assets would be reported as £2774m arrived at by adding current assets to fixed and others but leaving out of account the current labilities. These, in fact, appear, in the US system, added together with the equity and long-term loans. Thus ICI's equity and debt in the British system amount to £2143m, but in the American system amount to £2143m *plus* £631m, which, of course, equals the total assets (USA style) of £2774m. I shall have to use the US system (which always seems the more logical to me) for all calculations of Altman's Z, so let me make the difference between these two definitions quite clear in this simple table.

ICI's total assets in 1973 (£m)

UK system			*US system*		
Current assets	1330		Current assets	1330	
Current liabilities	−631				
Fixed and others	1444		Fixed and others	1444	
Total assets		2143	Total assets		2774
Equity and loans	2143		Equity and loans	2143	
			Current liabilities	631	
Total assets		2143	Total assets		2774

X_2 is retained earnings/total assets. Retained earnings is the total sum of profits that the company has retained over its lifetime. The shorter the life the less fat it will have accumulated and, probably, the lower this ratio. It may seem unfair that the equation will give a young company a weaker score for Z; but, as we have seen, most bankruptcies *are* of young companies.

X_3 is earnings before interest and taxes/total assets. It is simply our old friend 'return on capital employed' which is a measure of the pre-tax profits earned on all capital employed regardless of whether it is ordinary, preferred, loan or whatever. (But, note, it is the US definition of total assets.)

X_4 is market value of equity/book value of total debt. Here, for the first time, we have a non-accounting measure, namely the stock market capitalization. All the other ratios in Altman's equation are based on book values. So a company with ten million ordinary shares standing at $5 and a million preference at $4 will have a market value of $54m. As for the debt, here you take long-term *and* current debts.

X_5 is sales/total assets. This is that very common ratio of capital to turnover used by managers for years past.

So there is the equation. You work out these five ratios for your company, multiply each by its own constant, add them up, and arrive at Z, the figure which shows if your company is going bust. If Z is less than 1·8 you are almost certain to go bust, if it is more than 3·0 you almost certainly will not. Notice that the equation demands that *all* these ratios are used together and that the weighting given to each is maintained by using the right constant. Let us do a simple example.

Bankruptcy prediction—an example

The total assets of Hypothetics Limited is $1 500 000. Current assets are $500 000 and fixed and others are $1 000 000. Six hundred thousand $1 ordinary shares have been issued, which the stock exchange values at 50 cents each, and long-term loans amount to $400 000. Earnings so far retained total $100 000, current liabilities are $400 000 and this year a loss of $50 000 has been made on a turnover of $900 000. The five ratios are as follows:

X_1 = working capital/total assets = 100 000/1 500 000 = 6·7 per cent.
X_2 = retained earnings/total assets = 100 000/1 500 000 = 6·7 per cent.
X_3 = earnings before tax and interest/total assets = −50 000/1 500 000 = −3·3 per cent.

X_4 = market value/total debts = 300 000/800 000 = 37·5 per cent.
X_5 = sales/total assets = 900 000/1 500 000 = 60·0 per cent.

Now apply the co-efficients so the full equation becomes:

$$Z = 0{\cdot}012 \times 6{\cdot}7 + 0{\cdot}014 \times 6{\cdot}7 - 0{\cdot}033 \times 3{\cdot}3 + 0{\cdot}006 \times 37{\cdot}5 + 0{\cdot}01 \times 60{\cdot}0$$
$$= 0{\cdot}08 + 0{\cdot}09 - 0{\cdot}11 + 0{\cdot}23 + 0{\cdot}6 = 0{\cdot}89$$

So, according to the model, Hypothetics is well on its way to the bankruptcy courts for its Z, at about 0·9, is well below the 1·8 minimum. Altman has calculated that there is an area of uncertainty between this minimum 1·8 (below which it is extremely likely that a company will fail) and 3·0 (above which it pretty definitely will not). The best cut-off point to use is 2·675 but, of course, one is more in danger of misclassifying firms in this grey area. Using this equation Altman reckons to be able to predict 95 per cent correctly for firms that will fail within one year, and 72 per cent within two years. The accuracy falls off seriously after that; only 48 per cent within three years and about 30 per cent for four and for five years ahead. Exhibit 4.1 (p. 59) is of very considerable interest for it shows how a number of ratios (including the five that go into calculating Z) moved in the five years before bankruptcy of the 33 companies that Altman studied. Notice how sharply some of these changed for the worse between the third and second year from failure—this can also be seen by the graphs (Exhibit 4.2) I have reproduced from Altman's book. In Exhibit 4.3 I have calculated how Z moves using the five ratios shown in Exhibit 4.1. Notice how this composite Z for the 33 companies falls to below 1·8 approximately $2\frac{1}{2}$ years before bankruptcy.

One point that Altman finds interesting is the behaviour of stock market investors towards suspect firms. He believes that investors underestimate the plight of firms which eventually go bankrupt. He quotes some results of Professor William Beaver who in 1966 studied the dividend record and market price of shares of firms in two groups, bankrupt and non-bankrupt. He wanted a simple indicator for return on shareholder's capital so he added the dividends and stock market price together to give the 'return' and took the price on the base date as 'capital'. (So if you paid $100 for some shares which gave you a dividend of $2 in the first year, then one in the second year of $3 and you then sold them for $125, Beaver would say your return on your capital would have been 30 per cent.) Beaver found that, compared with the general stock market performance, the return on the bankrupt companies was worse than the non-failed for *five*

Exhibit 4.1. Average ratios for 33 bankrupt companies

Ratio	Fifth year Ratio	Fifth year Change[a]	Fourth year Ratio	Fourth year Change[a]	Third year Ratio	Third year Change[a]	Second year Ratio	Second year Change[a]	First year Ratio	First year Change[a]
	Years prior to failure									
Working capital/total assets (%) (X_1)	19·5		23·2	+3·6	17·6	−5·6	1·6	−16·0[b]	(6·1)	−7·7
Retained earnings/total assets (%) (X_2)	4·0		(0·8)	−4·8	(7·0)	−6·2	(30·1)	−23·1	(62·6)	−32·5[b]
EBIT/total assets (%) (X_3)	7·2		4·0	−3·2	(5·8)	−9·8	(20·7)	−14·9[b]	(31·8)	−11·1
Market value equity/total debt (%) (X_4)	180·0		147·6	−32·4	143·2	−4·4	74·2	69·0[b]	40·1	34·1
Sales/total assets (%) (X_5)	200·0		200·0	0·0	166·0	−34·0[b]	150·0	−16·0	150·0	0·0
Current ratio (%)	180·0		187·0	+7·0	162·0	−25·0	131·0	−31·0[b]	133·0	+2·0
Years of negative profits (yrs.)	0·8		0·9	+0·1	1·2	+0·3	2·0	+0·8[b]	2·5	+0·5
Total debt/total assets (%)	54·2		60·9	+6·7	61·2	+0·3	77·0	+15·8	96·4	+19·4[b]
Net worth/total debt (%)	123·2		75·2	−28·0	112·6	+17·4	70·5	−42·1[b]	49·4	−21·1

a. Change from previous year.
b. Largest yearly change in the ratio.

Source: Altman, *Corporate Bankruptcy in America*.

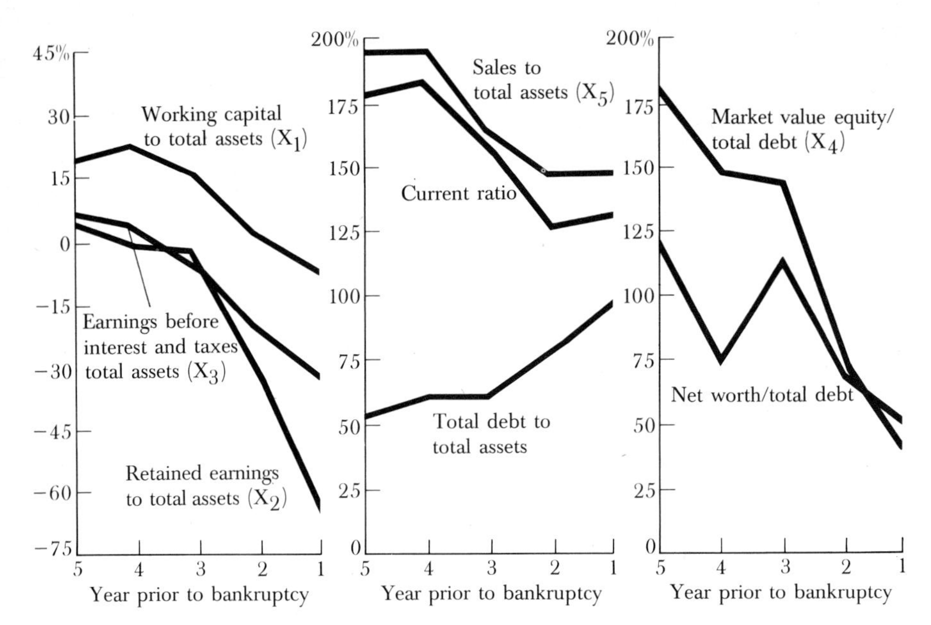

Exhibit 4.2. Source: Altman, *Corporate Bankruptcy in America.*

years prior to bankruptcy and that the difference in performance became progressively more marked as failure approached. As a matter of fact, Beaver showed that other ratios (such as cash flow/total liabilities; net income/total assets; total debt/total assets and working capital/total assets) all showed good predictive ability—very nearly as good as the stock market rate of return which, on average, gave 2·45 years warning. In the final year before failure, the rate of return moves down strongly. So it appears that investors certainly know that something is wrong a year ahead, probably 2½ years and even five years. Altman told me, in correspondence concerning this chapter, that he does not think (as Beaver does) that bankruptcy can be predicted five years ahead.

More recently, Westerfield has developed an equation which shows that

Exhibit 4.3. Value of Altman's Z calculated from the five ratios (X_1 to X_5) shown in Exhibit 4.1

	Fifth year	Fourth year	Third year	Second year	First year
Z	3·6	3·3	2·4	0·86	−0·26

investors start to move the share price of bankrupts-to-be down, relative to the stock market as a whole, as much as 59 months before failure. This also shows, says Altman, that investors are aware of a firm's deteriorating position a long time prior to failure, and certainly in the year immediately prior to bankruptcy, but they consistently underestimate the seriousness of the situation.

Rolls-Royce: a test for Z

Now, if I have correctly understood Altman, it should be possible to predict the failure of almost any company at least one year ahead and probably $2\frac{1}{2}$. Certainly it should be possible retrospectively. So, knowing that Rolls-Royce went bust on 4 February 1971, we should be able to see, right back in the 1969 accounts or even in 1968, that its Z was dropping perilously close to 1·8 and then down, down to Goodness Knows What by 1970. Let us therefore now write out the 10-year record for each of the factors that go into Altman's Z, do the sums, and see what happens. Most of the data we need is in Exhibit 4.4, which is in turn derived from Exhibit 5.1 in the next chapter. In taking the figures from Exhibit 5.1, which is a 10-year summary of Rolls-Royce's annual published accounts, I have had to translate them into the definitions used in Altman's equations. So total assets in Exhibit 4.4 are calculated by adding current liabilities to the total assets shown in Exhibit 5.1. And what Rolls-Royce calls 'net current assets', Altman calls 'working capital'. Also, to get Altman's 'total debts' I have taken the sum of Rolls-Royce's debentures, loan stock, deferred liabilities, interests of outside shareholders and all the current liabilities. The only item needed in Altman's equations that is missing from Exhibit 4.4 is the market value of Rolls-Royce's shares which I have shown separately in Exhibit 4.5. It will be seen that these vary considerably within each year so there is some doubt which figure to take into the ratio that Altman calls X_4. I have taken a middle guess but we may have to recalculate Z using a spread of figures for the market capitalization to see what effect share values have on our overall conclusions.

Now turn to Exhibit 4.6 (p. 64) where I show each of Altman's five ratios and his Z for the 10 years. This is what happens: most of the ratios, including Z, fall from 1961 to 1962 then pick up again until 1966. In that year—which is when Rolls-Royce merged with Bristol (see next chapter)—all the ratios fell dramatically (except X_4) and Z plunged from around

Exhibit 4.4. Selected data from Rolls-Royce accounts (£m)

	1961	62	63	64	65	66	67	68	69	70
Working capital	36·2	34·0	40·3	47·3	49·6	67·7	51·9	112·8	103·7	56·1
Total assets (US definition)	111·7	111·6	102·4	106·8	122·1	277·8	319·1	349·1	341·5	267·1
Retained profits	22·6	24·8	27·7	25·7	28·9	30·8	36·4	40·6	34·0	−55·3
Profits for the year	3·6	3·6	7·1	7·2	8·3	10·8	18·5	24·0	15·1	−3·2
Total debts	68·1	65·8	53·7	55·9	67·9	176·7	195·3	198·8	197·7	212·2
Sales turnover	122·3	108·0	102·4	107·0	127·2	171·5	265·5	321·7	301·4	274·6

Exhibit 4.5. High and low share values for Rolls-Royce

Year	High (p)	Low (p)	Millions of shares issued	Approx. middle market value (£m)
1961	245	175	20·2	42
1962	209	113	20·2	32
1963	165	124	20·2	29
1964	196	116	25·2	39
1965	206	155	25·3	46
1966	265	191	47·7	108
1967	265	219	56·0	135
1968	278	208	66·3	161
1969	247	107	66·3	117
1970	126	37	66·3	53
1971	45	—	66·3	30

2·5 to 1·5. But for the next two years most of the ratios recovered somewhat to 1969 when there was a minor deterioration in some of them, including Z. Only in 1970 was there a further severe deterioration in Z, but by then losses were being made. Rolls-Royce went into liquidation early in 1971.

This is not very satisfactory. The value of Z is below 3·0, Altman's good health certificate, for the whole 10-year period; it falls well below 1·8 in 1966, which implies that Rolls-Royce should have failed very soon after—but Z then actually improves until bankruptcy is almost round the corner when, at last, in 1970, it falls. But let us not forget that not many experts even in 1970 were predicting that Rolls-Royce would collapse in 1971, so this test of Z is not an unmitigated disaster. Yet it is worrying and we should seek an explanation. One is that Rolls-Royce accounts did not accurately reflect the true position. In fact we know that the Inspectors believed the profits in 1969 were overstated by £2·3m (see chapter 5). Very well, let us recalculate X_3 for 1969 on a profit of £12·8m instead of £15·1m. This brings Z down from 1·88 to 1·76. So that's not it.

Perhaps I should have taken the lowest stock market valuation for 1969 (£70m) instead of my middle guess of £117m. That brings Z down by another 0·2, so now we may be getting somewhere. Nor is it cheating to take the lowest 1969 share value, because Rolls-Royce's shares were tending downwards all through 1969. Anyone who calculated Z towards the end of 1969 might have arrived at quite a low figure for Z. And by 1970 the shares were down still further, so anyone who calculated Z in 1970, especially if he also adjusted profits for Rolls-Royce's propensity

Exhibit 4.6. Altman's five ratios and 'Z' for Rolls-Royce derived from Exhibits 4.4 and 4.5

Ratio		1961		62		63		64		65		66		67		68		69		70	
		%		%		%		%		%		%		%		%		%		%	
X1	Working capital ÷ total assets ×0·012	32·4	0·39	30·4	0·37	39·4	0·47	44·3	0·53	40·6	0·49	24·3	0·29	16·3	0·20	32·3	0·39	30·3	0·36	21·0	0·25
X2	Retained profits ÷ total assets ×0·014	20·2	0·28	22·2	0·31	27·1	0·38	24·1	0·34	23·6	0·33	11·1	0·15	11·4	0·16	11·6	0·16	9·9	0·14	−20·7	−0·29
X3	Profit for year ÷ total assets ×0·033	3·2	0·11	3·2	0·11	6·9	0·23	6·7	0·22	6·8	0·22	3·9	0·13	5·8	0·19	6·9	0·23	4·4	0·15	−1·2	−0·04
X4	Market value ÷ total debts. ×0·006	61·6	0·37	48·6	0·29	54·0	0·32	69·8	0·42	67·7	0·41	61·1	0·37	69·1	0·41	80·9	0·48	59·2	0·35	25·0	0·15
X5	Sales ÷ total assets ×0·01	109	1·09	97	0·97	100	1·00	100	1·00	104	1·04	61·7	0·62	83·2	0·83	92·1	0·92	88·2	0·88	102·8	1·03
Z			2·24		2·05		2·4		2·51		2·49		1·56		1·79		2·18		1·88		1·1

to treat R&D as capital, might have arrived at a very low Z. What about 1968—was any deterioration in Z visible then? I do not think so; I cannot see any valid modification to the accounts or the stock market value or any other figure that would have pushed Z down in 1968 compared with 1967 rather than up.

The predictive value of Z

There are, however, a number of other possible mitigating factors. First, Altman does not claim 100 per cent success rate and Rolls-Royce could be one of the exceptions, particularly as Altman's equations were based on 33 companies whose assets ranged from $0·7m to $25·9m (see p. 55), so they may not work for very large or very small companies. Second, Rolls-Royce was receiving a government subsidy of £40m over the 1966–70 period during which it declared profits totalling £30m. It could be said that, in reality, Rolls-Royce made a £10m loss over those five years and if that was taken into the calculations the effect on Z would be quite impressive! Third, I have taken Altman's equations straight out of US business environment and assumed they will work without modification to UK business environment. That this may be an unwarrantable assumption is supported by the fact that several Z calculations I have made for other UK companies give the wrong answers. Thus, the Z for ICI in 1972 and 1973 was 2·1 and 2·3—well below Altman's good health certificate of 3·0. So was GEC which had a Z of 2·3 for 1973 and for 1974. Both companies were perilously near the 1·8 danger line. One company that was below it is Alfred Herbert with Zs of 1·3 and 1·5 for 1972 and 1973, and we know that Alfred Herbert has applied for financial aid from the government (see p. 36) but GEC and ICI most certainly have not applied for any such aid.

From these figures it looks as if the Z levels in UK are generally lower than US. Perhaps any Z_{UK} above 2·0 is healthy, while below 1·5 is a danger signal. But then we face the awkward fact that for 1972 and for 1973 British Leyland scores 2·4. No one would believe that British Leyland was then more healthy than ICI or GEC. (British Leyland's high score is largely caused by the ratio X_5. Sales turnover in these years totalled around £1300m and £1600m while assets (US definition) totalled £800m and £1000m. Thus the contribution of X_5 *on its own* to the total value of Z is 1·6.)

So there are a number of unsolved difficulties. One, already mentioned in connection with Rolls-Royce, is obtaining a figure for market capitalization. The shares of a quoted company can vary by a factor of two or three within a year, which would severely affect the value of Z. This can be advantageous, for if the stock market began marking down the shares of a suspect company this would of itself tend to bring the value of Z down, thus making prediction of failure more probable. But not all companies are quoted on a stock market—only one in 40 in UK—so what figure for capitalization does one use for them? Altman's answer is to use the book value. But if we do this for British Leyland this lifts the 1972 or 1973 value of Z to 2·5. That's the wrong direction!

One of the phenomena we have seen in the two earlier chapters is that companies in trouble almost always hide the fact by creative accounting. The problem we now have is quite simple, then: you can only calculate Z meaningfully if you are given figures that are reliable; if you are given distorted figures then your Z will be wrong and the conclusion you base on it will be misleading. So this is what we have: Z tells you if a firm is going bust; Z is based on figures from published accounts; firms that are going bust distort their published accounts! It is a vicious circle that makes Z look rather useless. But not only that, the truth can be distorted in company accounts due to government subsidies, due to inflation, due to crooked accountants, due to unrealistic transfer prices between subsidiaries, due to international differences in definitions, and so on indefinitely. So where does that leave Z?

When a banker lends money to a company, the decision is heavily dependent upon what the banker feels about the company and its top managers. It tends to be a somewhat subjective decision. This is in contrast to procedures developed in the credit industry where a fairly reliable set of criteria exists for deciding whether to lend money to individual consumers. Now, Altman certainly does not suggest that his equations, including those for Z, are as reliable as these, but he does suggest that they could be useful analytical tools to supplement a banker's personal opinion of client companies to whom he is considering making loans. Where a bank specializes in one section of industry, and there are now a great number of specialist secondary banks lending to retailers or chemical companies or railroads, then perhaps they could develop specialized equations—each section of industry having different equations and different critical levels for Z. Special means of obtaining reliable up-to-date information could be devised and this would give added confidence to the values of Z thus obtained.

Implications for managers

The importance of Z for managers of companies lies in the fact that, as we have seen in the previous chapters, managers often do not appreciate how serious their company's situation is becoming until, apparently quite suddenly, they find there is not enough in the till to pay the wages. Now, if they were to calculate Z for their company every few months, this would first establish a norm for the level of Z for their company and then, perhaps, it would act as a barometer warning them of impending storms. The equation will not tell the managers what is wrong—it is not designed to—but it should tell them to start looking round for trouble and putting it right rather than going blindly on with some favourite project or other instead of manning the pumps.

Altman says there are six things managers can choose to do if they get a poor Z reading.

1. Change the product line or management personnel.
2. Sell off unprofitable equipment, plants or even entire divisions.
3. Solicit a takeover by a healthy company.
4. Alter the financial structure (debt or equity).
5. Bankruptcy-reorganization.
6. Liquidation.

Altman makes some extremely interesting points on all these possible actions. The first alternative, changes in products or people, can be successful in putting an ailing company back on a course of expansion, but this is very rare. Usually the approach of failure is recognized so late that something very much more radical is required, or at least, if such changes are to be relied on, then the changes themselves must be deep and wide—it will certainly be insufficient merely to put through a few face-saving retirements or rejig the product packaging! Such cosmetic actions are inappropriate by several orders of magnitude. On the other hand, the sale of whole divisions of the company might be drastic enough so long as there are major changes in top management also—indeed it is precisely these actions that so often lead to the recovery of a company after a bankruptcy-reorganization. So why not do it before, says Altman. As to the sale of property, this can be remedial, but only if the sale is normal. If it is forced by impending insolvency then the full market value may well not be obtained. In view of the time it sometimes takes to find a buyer, the sale of property is a lifebelt that can only be used with a lengthy period of warning—which is just what you do not usually get.

A merger can succeed—but here there is the same snag. It takes a considerable effort of will on the part of the directors of the failing company to admit their failure far enough ahead to give time even to look for a suitable takeover, let alone put one through. And in this takeover they are virtually certain to lose their jobs. One well-known merger occurred when Douglas Aircraft were, in the opinion of their bankers, approaching severe financial difficulties. They persuaded Douglas to merge with McDonnel Aircraft with considerable success. So it can be done, but perhaps only with the help of an outsider.

Turning now to his fourth alternative, Altman reviews some of the financial measures a US company can take including 'creditor composition and extension' by which creditors agree to reduce their claims or to delay them, on the assumption that they might then get something later instead of nothing if the company was allowed to fail right away. Or there is the downward revaluation of assets (to make return on capital employed look better) or one can eliminate accumulated losses by charging the deficit against the capital surplus account. However, all these financial arrangements are useful only if the company really is likely to recover and move into a new area of profits. If this is not likely then these measures are not only useless but may be dishonest and possibly illegal.

The process of bankruptcy-reorganization under 'Chapter X' of the Bankruptcy Act in the US is interesting. Put simply, the creditors (usually) ask the courts to appoint a trustee or Receiver to run the company, often with its existing managers, and to put forward a plan for its future which, if approved by a majority of each class of creditors, is then approved by the court. All the assets of the company are protected by the court during this process and it may borrow money on behalf of the firm. Very often a completely viable company emerges, although, of course, much changed and smaller, and not without losses to creditors, managers and employees as well as to the original shareholders, who often lose everything. Altman gives several examples of companies that have been to the verge of failure and then recovered in one or other of the six ways listed above. He mentions Muntz TV, for example, which expanded very rapidly from 1950 to

1954 and then was hit by a fall in TV sales and shortage of capital due to over-expansion. There was, by 1954, a total book net worth of minus $4m. But it occurred to the trustees that Muntz was not a failure and that the book values were misleading; so they sold off all Muntz's retail outlets, modernized the factories, claimed back overpaid tax, changed the top ten managers, and remodelled the finances. Profits were then made, rising to $850 000 in 1960 and 1961 and even the shareholders' equity realized a favourable return.

While Muntz found the way out through bankruptcy-reorganization, the North-eastern Steel Corporation found it through a merger while in bankruptcy-reorganization. This company was incorporated in 1954, the factory started up in 1955, and, having made nothing but losses, went into bankruptcy in 1957. The causes of this rapid disaster included under-estimating capital requirements for construction and start up, problems with suppliers and equipment, production cost escalation, and high interest rates due to over-gearing—they had $4·4m equity and $12·8m mortgage bonds and subordinated debentures! (That management persuaded people to subscribe to such gearing is interesting—as Altman says, 'somehow the promoters were able to secure financing from creditors who were willing to invest in a firm whose debt-to-total-assets ratio was 75% at its outset'.) Anyhow, the end of the story is that the trustees, having struggled on for at least a year, decided that the existing management was inefficient and inexperienced and the only hope was a merger. This was achieved eventually, partly helped by tax loss advantages to the acquiring company, so something at least was saved from the wreck.

I do not think there is any doubt about Altman's message to managers. It is that they have a duty to shareholders, to themselves, to employees and to the community to avoid the worst consequences of failure. This means doing two things that managers hardly ever do:

1. Watch out for the symptoms of failure.
2. If you see them, act.

If you just leave it, the consequences get worse as failure approaches.

Interim conclusions

I have extracted from Altman's book only those sections that are of direct relevance to corporate collapse and I have ignored completely several of his chapters such as those dealing with tax implications, mergers and railroad bankruptcies (although I do summarize his views on Penn Central in chapter 6). Even so, Altman has revealed to us a number of new facets of the subject of failure which I will now summarize. Later on, I will bring these interim conclusions together with all the others in this book to try to form a full consensus.

FACTS AND FIGURES

Statistics on failure in America suggest that out of 4·5 million businesses that are registered about nine per cent cease trading and 10 per cent start up during an average year. Only about 0·4 per cent actually fail—about one in 250—and the failure rate, which is expressed as the number of failures per 10 000, is around 40. Of those that fail, only two per cent are a year old or less, but well over half are less than five years old. About 20 per cent are more than 10 years old. As to causes, there are a great number of them and unfortunately, human nature being what it is, the causes listed by failed owners differ so much from the list put forward by the creditors that analysing causes is not a very useful exercise. It is far more sensible to try to predict failure far enough ahead to do something about it.

PREDICTING FAILURE

A number of attempts have been made to develop methods of prediction. Some experts in US, such as Beaver and Westerfield, rely on normal ratio analysis, using cash flow/debt and other fairly well-known ratios or they use stock market indices. Some claim that failure can be seen five years ahead by such means but Altman thinks two years is more like it. He prefers not to rely on single ratios but to develop equations (using MDA) which involve a number of ratios each contributing its own weighted influence to the conclusion. He looks at factors that lie outside the firm as well as inside.

EXTERNAL FACTORS

Three factors seem particularly important. The change in GNP is one. Failure rates rise at the same time, or perhaps just before, a fall in GNP.

The other two, which move at virtually the same time as failure rate, are stock market performance, and money supply. Oddly enough, neither failure rate nor failure liabilities seemed to be linked strongly with the trend in corporate profits—certainly not as strongly as many people believe. Failure liabilities were less closely linked to GNP and stock market than failure rate, but did seem to be linked to the number of firms in existence. Money supply did not seem to influence failure liabilities at all, perhaps because credit is available to big firms even in periods of credit restriction, but it is big firms that influence the failure liability statistics. The equations developed by Altman to show the influence of these external factors on failure are appropriate only to the US, of course.

INTERNAL FACTORS

Five internal ratios are important. These are the working capital, retained earnings, current profits and sales, all expressed as ratios of the total assets, and the market value as a ratio to debt. These all contribute to Z, which indicates a company's propensity to fail, a score of less than 1·8 being extremely bad, while a score of more than 3·0 suggests continued viability.

Altman himself suggests that this calculation is probably too general and that it would be preferable to calculate Z scores for each sector of industry in each national economy. Certainly the test given to Z here, using Rolls-Royce, was not very satisfactory although it must be admitted that Rolls-Royce's Z score in 1970 would have been low enough to arouse real anxiety in anyone who had calculated it.

PREVENTION AND CURE

Altman suggests that companies that are in some difficulty should take urgent action if there is reason to think that an economic downturn or credit squeeze is on the way. As to what one can do to avert disaster, there are six courses open. To *change the product or the management*—but this is useless unless the changes are really radical. To *sell off unprofitable parts*—if there is time. To *solicit a takeover*—again, if there is time. To *alter the financial structure*—but not if it is intended merely to deceive. To *petition for bankruptcy-reorganization*. To *go into liquidation*.

Of course, the company will take none of these remedial actions unless the management are already doing something that not many managers do: keeping watch on the propensity of their company to failure, perhaps by monitoring their Z scores.

5. *Rolls-Royce*

Precisely when Great Britain's economy began to decline relative to the rest of the world is a matter for debate. Some people say that Britain was exhausted by the Second World War and so the decline began in 1940, but others look right back to the 1880s. Over this period of many decades, few events could have dealt such a savage shock to the confidence of the British people as the collapse of Rolls-Royce on 4 February 1971. Rolls-Royce was the symbol of effortless power and smooth efficiency, Rolls-Royce was the pinnacle of British quality and workmanship; and now Rolls-Royce was as broke, bust and well and truly bankrupt as any back-street builder. The whole world gasped in amazement.

It should not be too difficult to determine why Rolls-Royce failed, for in addition to the Official Report from the Inspectors, Messrs MacCrindle and Godfrey, which runs to 400 pages, a large number of commentators have expressed their varied views. What I hope to do in this chapter is to describe the Rolls-Royce failure in some detail and examine the symptoms and causes and the preventative measures that Rolls-Royce might have taken. This is to verify whether the lists we have built up over the past three chapters have any validity for Rolls-Royce—it will be recalled that in chapter 2 we tried to do the same thing in the case of Stirling Homex. But on that occasion it was most unsuccessful for very few of the items in the writer's lists featured significantly in that particular real-life example. If we do not do better in the case of Rolls-Royce we will have to consider whether these lists are any use at all.

So the whole purpose of this chapter is to see how many elements that are said to be associated with failure were actually present in this case. The sole reason I have taken Rolls-Royce as our guinea-pig is that it is probably the best-documented case study available (along with Penn Central, described in the next chapter), so one hopes that most of the salient facts will be correct. The story covers a whole decade and as it is rather complicated I have broken it up into sections, as does the Official Report upon which I have heavily relied. In the last sections of this chapter I shall review a number of expert opinions on the causes, symptoms and prevention. Before we look at Rolls-Royce's last decade I should briefly review its earlier history.

The company was started in 1906, with a capital of £60 000, by the Hon. C. S. Rolls and Henry Royce who had met for the first time in 1904. The company was to 'make, sell, let on hire . . . motor vehicles for use on land or water or in the air . . .' and their first product, the Silver Ghost car, was the foundation-stone of the business. The quality of its design and of its workmanship was unrivalled and demand was so great that the company quickly outgrew Royce's factory at Manchester and moved to larger premises in Derby. Thus the company was well and truly established before the 1914–18 war, when it was not entirely surprising to find Rolls-Royce switching to aero-engines. Royce's first engine, the Eagle, powered a number of war planes, and, in 1919, took Alcock and Brown across the Atlantic. Then came the 'R' aero-engine, a V.12 which powered the record-breaking Supermarine seaplane in 1931 and, later on, powered record-breaking vehicles on land and water as well. Then came the Merlin which, as every schoolboy knows, was fitted in the Spitfire and Hurricane. Also in 1931 Rolls-Royce absorbed the Bentley car company, which was in financial difficulties, but by this date Rolls-Royce was no longer a car company but an aero-engine company. That was true in 1931; it was even more so in 1945.

Indeed, the end of the Second World War brought a major strategic dilemma for Rolls-Royce. Most of its 47 000 employees in 1945 were making engines for warplanes and it was a measure of the looming strategic problem that within 15 months of the end of the war this was down to half—24 000. What should they do? Aero-engine demand would surely continue to fall and there was no guarantee that the demand for luxury cars would ever return. Should they diversify? The decision they made was not to diversify but to build on their undoubted ability and reputation by aiming for a large share of the high quality, high technology aero-engine market, including of course jet engines, and to return to the manufacture of luxury cars. The Welland, the only Allied jet engine to go into service during the war, thus became the foundation stone for Rolls-Royce's post-war strategy—and a highly successful strategy it was, too.

From the Welland came the Nene, the Tay, the Dart, Tyne, Avon, Conway and Spey. By the early sixties, more than half of all jet-engined civil aircraft in the Western world were powered by Rolls-Royce. By the late sixties there were 90 000 employees, the company had become *the* leading aero-engine company in Europe, it was the twenty-second largest industrial company in Britain, and its reputation, not only in engines but in many related branches of high technology, was world-wide.

The RB 178

It was against this background of a decade of success in this highly specialized field that Rolls-Royce began, in 1961, to think seriously about a new large engine of advanced design. Work began on it—it was called the RB 178—in 1963. It had two shafts, a high by-pass ratio and was to develop 25 000 lb thrust. By 1965 they had built a 'demonstrator'—a pre-production version on which the development engineers could bring performance up to design specification—and in July 1966 it ran at 93 per cent of power. But these tests showed up some rather serious design faults. Also in July 1966 work began on the Trent engine which was to have three shafts. And very soon afterwards all work on the RB 178 was stopped.

It was stopped because of lack of finance. Rolls-Royce was feeling the financial strains of a heavy R&D programme. The consequences of this decision—'one of our great mistakes', as Sir David Huddie later admitted—were severe, because it was from this engine concept that the RB 211 was to be developed. Had development of the RB 178 continued, then some of the problems that were met in the RB 211 might have been solved as much as two years earlier, according to some of Rolls-Royce's engineers. The UK government contributed £1·3m to the RB 178 programme.

It had been Rolls-Royce's hope that the RB 178 would have been suitable for Boeing's Jumbo Jet. That Boeing's chose an American engine (a Pratt and Whitney) was not really very surprising. For one thing, no nation—and certainly not one that prides itself on its technology—likes to buy foreign jet engines. This is an emotion that the US government effectively backed with 'Buy American' regulations at that time. But another reason was that both Pratt and Whitney and the other US jet engine manufacturer, General Electric, were now years ahead of Rolls-Royce in the development of big engines, thanks largely to the financial backing given to them by the US government to develop engines for the huge military transport plane known as the C5A.

The RB 211

Let us consider the strategic situation at the time it was decided to go ahead with the RB 211. A market survey had shown two things. One was that a very large volume of demand for very large jet engines was developing world-wide, but especially in the US, as a result of the trend in design towards wide-bodied airliners. The other was that the demand for the five engines then being made by Rolls-Royce would fall rapidly. Indeed it was thought that sales of these engines would have fallen from their then (1965) level of £100m to as low as £3m per annum by 1975! Nor were things looking any brighter on the technical side for, as suggested above, Rolls-Royce was now some years behind the Americans in big engine technology. It is impossible to say now what course Sir Denning Pearson (chief executive from 1957–70) should have chosen for Rolls-Royce at this point in its history. What he actually did was to decide, on the strength of Rolls-Royce's remarkable engineering ability, to carry the war directly into the enemy camp. His strategy was: *build a big engine and sell it to the Americans.* It was bold and daring. But there was nothing else in prospect that could conceivably fill the huge hole that was predicted to appear in Rolls-Royce's turnover in the next decade.

In taking this course, Sir Denning must have had in mind Rolls-Royce's legendary ability as engineers. And did they not have no less than three technological tricks up their sleeve that would astonish the Americans? There was the three-shaft concept, the annular combustion chamber and Hyfil instead of titanium for the turbine blades. MacCrindle and Godfrey say in the Official Report that in launching into this most challenging project there was in fact 'no special cause for confidence'. The Tyne was not a success, although it cost £17m to develop; the Medway was cancelled, and the Trent (mentioned above) was cancelled. The Spey was successful, but its development cost £30m up to 1962 when it went into service.

It was in this strategic situation, then, that it was decided to go ahead with the RB 211. In 1967 it was expected to cost £60m to develop, of which the government agreed to put up approximately 70 per cent (instead of their usual 50 per cent), or £40m. The return on this investment was expected to be massive; Rolls-Royce hoped to sell over 3000 engines at £¼m each for a turnover of £860m in the decade 1970–79 and to make a profit of £264m (before loan interest). Bearing in mind that when these figures were first put forward (1967) Rolls-Royce's annual turnover was £300m and profits £20m (see Exhibit 5.1 on page 84), it was clear that the RB 211 was intended to become an enormous proportion of the total Rolls-Royce organization.

At this stage in the story I believe a few words of explanation are required. I myself found it almost inconceivable that the development of a jet engine, however large, could possibly cost £60m or that it could cost nearly £¼m to build each production unit. As every tourist knows, a jet engine is just a couple of big fans with an oil burner in between. But let no one underestimate the level of perfection required in this branch of engineering. Consider only the matter of reliability, for example, where these engines have to fly four million miles between overhauls. To develop such machinery you need high-speed cameras, flying test-beds, high altitude test facilities and vacuum pits. You have to test to destruction, you have to redesign and respecify not just any component that is faulty but many of its contingent components—and to design just one component you may need 60 skilled men working for several months. As for the production line: these engines are not mass produced—they are virtually hand made, and each new batch has a dozen improvements or modifications more than the last batch. And if it is still inconceivable that Rolls-Royce could spend £60m on the development of the RB 211 it might be worth noting that to develop the engine for the C5A, General Electric spent $450m (every cent of it from the US government). In view of this—and let us not forget that the Spey cost £30m nearly a decade before—the 1967 estimate of £60m begins to look what it was—hopelessly inadequate!

To return to the sequence of events. In June 1967 Rolls-Royce made its offer on price and delivery for the RB 211 to Lockheeds. Delivery of the first few engines was to be made in 1971. (It might be noted that this is a four-year development period. It might have been noted, on page 75, that it took five years to bring the RB 178 from concept to demonstrator.) In December 1967 the Trent ran successfully, thus proving the three-shaft concept for the first time. So that was one technical triumph. The second technical leap, the Hyfil blades, were successful in normal conditions but were found to be insufficiently impact-resistant to birds ingested into the engine in flight and Rolls-Royce eventually had to develop titanium blades at considerable extra cost to themselves.

In March 1968 the contract with Lockheed was signed amid wild jubilation in Rolls-Royce, in Parliament and in the Press. It was indeed a massive victory—but more of the details later. In July 1968 the first RB 211 ran on test and was seen to be substantially below specification. Six months later, in January 1969 the main board were told that 'the engine is not anywhere near its performance . . .'. But it is now misleading to talk about 'the' engine because by then there were two. One, the RB 211–06 was so far from the required specification that they had almost started again with a new version called the RB 211–22. In April 1969 it was estimated that this engine would cost about 12½ per cent more than the original estimate two years earlier but this fact was not reported to the board. What they were now told was that the engine had demonstrated full thrust on test and that 'the total task is still a formidable one but it is, we believe, achievable'. The Inspectors say in their paragraph 354 that this may have been so but the board were also not told that this full thrust was only achieved at a much higher temperature than specified.

By June 1969 the launch costs were estimated at £100m compared with the original (June 1967) of £60–70m. But on top of this came the Metcalfe Report. I should explain that Rolls-Royce was managed by a main board of which Sir Denning Pearson was the chief executive and, responsible to this board, there were several subsidiary companies each of which also had a board. One of these subsidiaries was the Derby Engine Division (DED), of which the chief executive was Sir David Huddie. It was DED who were developing the RB 211 and the man in charge of the project was Mr Metcalfe. He now reported to his board (DED) that the cost of each engine would probably be £187 744 instead of £153 655 as estimated in 1968. Consequently there would be a loss of £16·3m on the RB 211–22 project instead of a profit of £46·9m as previously believed.

This adverse swing of a cool £63m was not reported to the main board, nor according to the inspectors (paragraph 359) were any of Mr Metcalfe's remarks.

Meanwhile engine testing was going ahead and reports to the DED board continued to highlight further technical troubles, delays and overspending. In September 1969 Sir David told the main board that the RB 211 programme was being put on an emergency basis. In November Mr Metcalfe was at it again: he told Sir David that unless some very special steps were taken, 'we will not have an engine that works at all'.

In March 1970 a Hyfil fan blade failed and the engine virtually exploded. Hyfil was then abandoned and titanium was used, making a further addition of weight to the engine which was already overweight. In that month launch costs were now estimated to be £135m (compared with £100m at the June 1969 estimate) and each engine was expected to cost £205 380 (compared with Mr Metcalfe's June 1969 estimate of £187 744). A few days later (yes, days) a new estimate showed launch costs of £151m and each engine to cost £217 338. In May the various test engines ran for 125 hours instead of the planned 360 because of the many technical problems. And now Lockheed wanted the first few engines delivered in November for early flight trials of the TriStar, and it was Rolls-Royce's frantic efforts to meet this deadline that drew resources away from the development programme. By a miracle, these engines, nowhere near the required reliability it is true, were handed over only three weeks late and they delivered enough thrust to allow TriStar to start flight tests.

Indeed, by the end of the year it looked as though all the technical problems would be overcome, although certainly not within the contractual period and at enormous extra cost. Serious thought was given to asking Lockheeds for a delay. In January 1971 a new estimate showed launch costs at £203m and each engine at £281 000. Further engineering problems emerged as the testing programme pushed the engine nearer its design limits and several engines failed. It was now abundantly clear that disaster was at hand.

By some freak of fate one of the engines tested late in the evening of 3 February came so close to meeting the thrust specification that the jubilant engineer sent a telex to the London office on 4 February. It was only a few hours later that the Receiver was called in.

It is a somewhat happier task to trace the RB 211 saga a few years further on. For, having risen from the ashes, Rolls-Royce (1971) Ltd had, by July 1974, delivered 350 engines for a turnover of £200m. The total sales will easily exceed £1000m and the RB 211 could well be Rolls-Royce's major product line for two or three decades, finding application not only in aircraft but in marine and industrial uses all over the world.

The Lockheed contract

The strategic decision that Sir Denning had made was for Rolls-Royce to develop a big engine and sell it to the Americans. That meant persuading an American aircraft manufacturer to install Rolls-Royce engines as standard in the original aircraft including those flying with American airlines. Previously Rolls-Royce engines had only been fitted in those American-built aircraft that flew with European or other airlines—never as a standard fitting in America. As we have seen, Rolls-Royce failed to persuade Boeing to adopt the RB 178 as standard in 1966. But Boeing's Jumbo Jet was only the first in a long line of the new wide-bodied airliners such as the TriStar from Lockheed, the Douglas DC 10, the BAC 2–11, the European Airbus, all of which would be powered by two or three of the new generation of big jets. Clearly there was plenty to go for.

Lockheed asked Rolls-Royce to submit a quotation to them for the RB 211 for their TriStar by 16 January 1967. Unfortunately, it took some time for the British government to decide what form their financial help for this project would take, but by 23 June Rolls-Royce sent off their quotation. The price for each installed engine (the basic engine plus accessories) would be $450 900 (then equal to £193 000) with delivery starting in 1971. The specification of the engine to be supplied was extremely complex, as one would expect, but among the figures mentioned was a thrust of 33 260 lb. On 20 July, Rolls-Royce sent a similar quotation to Douglas for their DC 10.

From that point onwards the volume of information exchanged between Lockheed and Rolls-Royce grew rapidly. Lockheed wanted more thrust, Rolls-Royce would quote a higher price, sterling was devalued, Rolls-Royce quoted a revised price, this acoustic material would be used, that fan blade would be like this, the thrust reversers would do that, still more thrust was needed, another $10 000 would go on the price, the engine mountings. . . . Meanwhile the two American engine manufacturers were not standing idly by watching Rolls-Royce take their market from them. A vigorous battle was joined. General Electric cut the price of their engine by three per cent, Rolls-Royce followed suit. Sir David moved to America to join his sales team there and, in trying conscientiously to carry out the job of chief executive of DED at the same time very nearly killed himself.

The pressure to sell this engine was immense. Not only did the whole future of Rolls-Royce depend upon the outcome but the British government were uttering patriotic noises of encouragement all the time. The boost that success would give to national morale, not to mention the balance of payments, was obvious. On 28 March 1968 all these efforts were crowned with success—the contract with Lockheeds was signed! The terms were, of course, now very different from those in the original quotation nine months before. The thrust required was now 39 576 lb—up by 19 per cent. The price was now $565 000—up by 4½ per cent—but that was the price to Lockheed. The price to Rolls-Royce in sterling had risen to £235 000—up 22 per cent due to devaluation. Nevertheless, there is no doubt that in the deal enshrined in the contract Rolls-Royce was giving more for less compared with their quotation. The contract itself contained some very tough clauses, as all contracts signed under conditions of tough competition are likely to. In particular there were some severe penalties for late delivery and cancellation and the provisions for escalation due to cost inflation were minimal.

There was something else. Rolls-Royce had decided, right back at the beginning of their discussion with Lockheed, not to go ahead with the RB 211 unless *at least* two American airlines were committed to order the TriStar. The reasoning behind this was that experts believed then that there was only room for one wide-bodied airliner in the American market. If three airlines were to order the TriStar all the others would too; if only two ordered the TriStar then there was still a chance that the others would go for the DC 10 thus creating an intolerable level of competition for a decade. But now caution was thrown to the winds and the contract was signed even though it was known that at least one airline had already ordered the DC 10. The DC 10 was to be fitted with General Electric engines.

The rôle of the government

Even in those nations where the civil airlines are not state-owned, the state always takes an active and important part in regulating the running of national airlines. The state always dominates and finances the only other major aircraft market, namely the military one. So if you build aircraft or parts for aircraft or have anything whatever to do with aircraft then, like it or not, your relationship with governments will be vital. And, vice versa, whenever a great success occurs in the aircraft industry, or a great failure, it is relevant to ask what part the government played in it.

Relations between the UK government and Rolls-Royce were certainly close. Throughout the post-war period a continuous exchange of views took place between ministers and civil servants and the top management of Rolls-Royce. It is of particular relevance to the collapse of Rolls-Royce that Lord Kindersley (chairman 1957–68), Sir Denning and Sir David all wrote at length on long-term policy, on technology and on finance throughout the sixties. There was, for example, no misunderstanding as to the terms of the government's launching aid for the RB 211. The government would give Rolls-Royce £40m out of the £60·25m that they estimated it would cost for research and development. The figure was £40m and not a penny more—not even if launching costs rose, as indeed they did. So it was fully understood that if launching costs came to £70m then Rolls-Royce would have to put up £30m of their own money and if they came to £100m then they would have to find £60m. In the event, when costs did rise, the government relented and offered another £42m—but by then Rolls-Royce was beyond help. In the matter of the launching aid, therefore, I believe the government cannot be criticized.

In two other respects it can. One is the traditional meanness of UK governments towards the aircraft industry. While other governments (US, France, Sweden, etc.) give hundreds of millions of pounds to ensure that their civil and military aircraft industries are internationally competitive, the UK government gives mere tens of millions. By this attitude the government may well have contributed to the long-term decline of the industry as a whole and to Rolls-Royce in particular. But, on the other hand, this lack of generosity has always been the case and Rolls-Royce must have been as aware of this fact as anyone. It was certainly a fact that should have been taken into account when they built their bold and daring strategy around the RB 211 project.

The other ground for criticism is that the government does appear to have encouraged Rolls-Royce in this huge project knowing full well that it would stretch the company to bursting point. This was one of the matters raised by the Inspectors when they interviewed Sir Denning but he denies ever having believed that the government would rescue Rolls-Royce if it got into serious trouble. I confess that in Sir Denning's place I would have been sorely tempted to believe it. After all, Rolls-Royce went after that Lockheed contract not only for its own salvation but certain in the knowledge that success would significantly contribute to the UK balance of payments—the government had said so time and again. I would have believed that the government would bale them out, and I do not think that Sir Denning—or the banks, or the debenture holders, or anyone else—could have been blamed if they had thought so too.

The Bristol merger

As a result of government policy there were only two aero-engine manufacturers left in Britain by 1960, Rolls-Royce and Bristol Siddeley, just as there were only two airframe manufacturers and one helicopter manufacturer. Rolls-Royce could not have been too pleased when the contract to supply the engines for Concorde went to Bristol. Sir Denning was certainly not pleased when he heard reports in December 1965 that Bristol was about to form some sort of association with Pratt and Whitney concerning the development of a big engine—precisely the market area that Rolls-Royce was about to enter—quite apart from giving an American manufacturer direct access into the European market. In March 1966 Rolls-Royce began discussing a possible merger with Bristol and the deal was agreed and put into effect before the end of the year.

Under the merger terms, Rolls-Royce paid Bristol's shareholders £63·6m. Of this, £37m was in Rolls-Royce shares and £26·6m in cash, which Rolls-Royce raised mainly from a £20m debenture issue. This figure of £63·6m was made up of £41·7m for the assets of Bristol plus £21·9m of 'goodwill' and it was justified by Bristol's forecast of their profits over the following three years. This forecast suggested a figure of £20m for the years 1966–68 so Rolls-Royce were effectively valuing Bristol at about 10 years' profits. Rolls-Royce later calculated that in fact Bristol had only contributed about £5m or £6m profits in those years and one might conclude that they therefore should only have paid approximately £20m for Bristol. To say this is to ignore the grave threat that Bristol's flirtation with Pratt and Whitney was to Rolls-Royce's whole strategy—

Exhibit 5.1. Rolls-Royce Ltd 1961–70. Profit and loss accounts and balance sheets

	Group									Company only
	1961 £m	1962 £m	1963 £m	1964 £m	1965 £m	1966 £m	1967 £m	1968 £m	1969 £m	1970 £m
Revenue from all sources	122·3	108·0	102·4	107·0	127·2	171·5	265·5	321·7	301·4	274·6
Cost of manufacture, selling and administration	112·4	99·7	90·7	95·2	113·5	153·9	241·3	291·3	276·0	266·9
	9·9	8·3	11·7	11·8	13·7	17·6	24·2	30·4	25·4	7·7
Research and development	6·3	4·7	4·6	4·6	5·4	6·8	5·7	6·4	10·3	10·9
	3·6	3·6	7·1	7·2	8·3	10·8	18·5	24·0	15·1	(3·2)
Interest charges	1·1	1·8	1·3	0·8	1·4	2·4	6·7	8·1	8·7	9·0
Profit (loss) before taxation	2·5	1·8	5·8	6·4	6·9	8·4	11·8	15·9	6·4	(12·2)
Taxation	—	—	1·8	2·8	2·4	3·1	4·2	7·0	2·0	3·2 (a)
	2·5	1·8	4·0	3·6	4·5	5·3	7·6	8·9	4·4	(9·0)
Profit attributable to outside shareholders of subsidiary companies	—	0·1	—	—	—	—	0·1	0·1	0·1	—
Profit (loss) after taxation attributable to Rolls-Royce	2·5	1·7	4·0	3·6	4·5	5·3	7·5	8·8	4·3	(9·0)
Dividends	1·0	0·7	1·2	1·5	1·6	3·7	6·1	7·3	4·0	—
	1·5	1·0	2·8	2·1	2·9	1·6	1·4	1·5	0·3	(9·0)
Special provisions on RB 211 less anticipated tax relief—										
Research and development	—	—	—	—	—	—	—	—	11·0	—
Future production losses	—	—	—	—	—	—	—	—	—	78·8
Transfer to (from) retained profits	1·5	1·0	2·8	2·1	2·9	1·6	1·4	1·5	(10·7)	(87·8)

Note (a)—Release from taxation equalization accounts

	Group 1961 £m	1962 £m	1963 £m	1964 £m	1965 £m	1966 £m	1967 £m	1968 £m	1969 £m	only 1970 £m
Current assets										
Cash and bank balances	0·5	0·6	0·7	0·4	0·4	0·7	0·7	1·1	0·9	1·7
Debtors	32·9	35·0	36·0	36·8	40·8	84·4	98·3	118·0	110·9	88·7
Stocks	49·1	44·2	36·7	43·6	53·7	108·6	124·6	115·6	112·1	105·2
	82·5	79·8	73·4	80·8	94·9	193·7	223·6	234·7	223·9	195·6
Current liabilities										
Bank indebtedness	11·7	18·3	11·9	9·0	15·3	26·0	41·3	32·4	37·0	44·6
Acceptances	9·3	10·0	5·0	1·7	4·0	15·0	15·0	14·0	17·0	18·0
Creditors	21·9	15·9	13·7	20·1	22·2	78·4	64·2	63·6	62·3	76·7
Taxation	3·0	0·9	1·3	1·6	2·5	3·7	7·1	6·8	1·9	0·2
Dividends	0·4	0·7	1·2	1·1	1·3	2·9	4·1	5·1	2·0	—
	46·3	45·8	33·1	33·5	45·3	126·0	131·7	121·9	120·2	139·5
Net current assets	36·2	34·0	40·3	47·3	49·6	67·7	51·9	112·8	103·7	56·1
Investments	0·8	1·2	1·5	0·2	0·1	9·9	7·3	7·7	6·9	25·0
Property and plant	21·8	22·9	21·2	20·6	21·8	43·2	55·2	69·8	82·5	83·7
Research and development	6·6	7·7	6·3	5·2	5·3	6·3	8·3	12·2	3·5	25·7
Goodwill, patents and trademarks	—	—	—	—	—	24·7	24·7	24·7	24·7	15·9
	65·4	65·8	69·3	73·3	76·8	151·8	187·4	227·2	221·3	206·4
Special provision for future production losses	—	—	—	—	—	—	—	—	—	(78·8)
	65·4	65·8	69·3	73·3	76·8	151·8	187·4	227·2	221·3	127·6
Issued share capital	20·2	20·2	20·2	25·2	25·3	47·7	56·0	66·3	66·3	66·3
Share premium account	0·8	0·8	0·8	—	—	22·6	31·4	43·4	43·5	43·5
Retained profits	22·6	24·8	27·7	25·7	28·9	30·8	36·4	40·6	34·0	(55·3)
	43·6	45·8	48·7	50·9	54·2	101·1	123·8	150·3	143·8	54·5
Debentures and loan stocks	15·7	15·6	15·4	15·1	14·9	38·6	48·6	57·2	56·7	65·1
Deferred liabilities	6·0	4·2	5·0	7·0	7·4	11·8	14·5	19.2	20·2	8·0
Interests of outside shareholders of subsidiary companies	0·1	0·2	0·2	0·3	0·3	0·3	0·5	0·5	0·6	—
	65·4	65·8	69·3	73·3	76·8	151·8	187·4	227·2	221·3	127·6

indeed it soon became known that Bristol had in fact signed heads of agreement with Pratt and Whitney (and Snecma, the French aero-engine company) so the threat was very real. I believe, and I think the Inspectors do too, that the merger was a purely defensive move by Rolls-Royce even though, at the time, a list of no less than 19 positive advantages was drawn up to justify it.

The Inspectors say of this merger that it was a shot-gun wedding and 'that the strains imposed on Rolls-Royce finances by the conjugal relationship did nothing to strengthen Rolls-Royce in its subsequent times of trial' but that, 'We do not consider that the acquisition or the burdens which it imposed on Rolls-Royce were causative of the later crash . . .'. But in another section of their report they note that until the merger Rolls-Royce had never paid out more than £2m in loan interest in any year while after it this figure rose to between £7m and £9m. But that is not all. In Exhibit 5.1 I reproduce a 10-year summary of Rolls-Royce's published accounts from which it can be calculated that, for example, their current assets doubled after the merger but their current liabilities trebled. Creditors increased from 9 or 10 weeks to 10 to 12 weeks (the figure for 1966 itself was 24 weeks but this must have been a freak, as some of the other figures for 1966 may have been, due to accounting differences in the two merging companies). Again, the acid test ratio was approximately unity before the merger but fell to 0·7 in 1966 and 1967. And we should not forget what the calculation of Altman's Z showed (p. 60). I find it hard to think of the Inspector's statement that the merger 'did nothing to strengthen Rolls-Royce' as anything but a splendid example of British understatement.

Finance

To follow this strand of the story it is necessary to look back to 1960. In that year the book value of Rolls-Royce was £60·9m and there was a debenture of £3·8 and bank borrowing, etc., of £9·7m. So in 1960, 22 per cent of their capital was borrowed money. In 1961 there were substantial stock losses, the Tyne engine development went awry and, all in all, it was a bad year. They had to raise £11·9m in debentures and nearly £10m in bank loans so that suddenly, in this single year, borrowings rose to 46 per cent of total capital—and it stayed at that level until the end. It may be thought that this level of gearing is too high for a company subjected to such high risk but apparently it was normal for the aircraft industry at that time.

During the same decade operating margins first rose (from 8 to 10 per cent) and then, from the mid-sixties fell again (to 8 per cent). Return on capital employed rose until the mid-sixties and then fell. Turnover, on the other hand, remained static for five years, rose after the merger until 1968 and then fell back again. As for profits before tax, they began the decade at £2m, rose to £7m before the merger, and then rose from £8m to £12m to £16m in 1968 before collapsing to £6m in 1969 and a loss of £12m in 1970.

These profit figures are quoted after deducting some, but not all, of the research costs incurred each year. Again we have to go back to 1960 for the start of this strange story. In 1960 the company's operating profit was a healthy £12·9m, out of which it was entirely possible to take the whole of the £7·7m research expenditure for the year and still leave £5·2m profits before tax to give a return on capital of 8·5 per cent; low, but acceptable. But 1961 was a thoroughly tiresome year for Rolls-Royce, with operating profits down to £9·9m and research costs up to £10·5m. That implies a loss of £1·7m after interest. The board decided to capitalize £4·2m of this quite exceptionally high research figure (in fact research expenditure dropped to around £5m from 1962 right up to 1966 and never came near £10m again until 1967) so they could show a profit of £2·5m after interest. In other words, out of an actual expenditure of £10·5m on R&D, only £6·3m was written off against current profits for 1962—and, while they were about it, the board also retrospectively capitalized another £2·4m out of the 1960 R&D expenditure of £7·7m.

The intention was to recover this capital investment from sales resulting from firm orders that had already been received for the engines under development but not yet executed. And this is in fact what was done. But in 1967, R&D expenditure began to rise again due to the RB 211 programme and this policy was changed slightly but significantly. As well as providing for recovery against firm orders already received they extended the policy to cover orders that they *expected* to receive. The extreme flexibility of interpretation that this introduced allowed them to capitalize some substantial amounts; in 1968, for example, R&D actually cost £14·1m, of which only £6·4m was charged to profits. For the whole decade, and especially from 1967 onwards, the assets of the company were being inflated and, worse, the profits were, too. Had R&D been written off as it was incurred—as is now generally recommended by the accountancy profession—the profits declared would not have covered the dividends that were paid in 1967, 1968 or 1969.

The last few months

Throughout 1969, as the company's technical staff became progressively more anxious about the RB 211, the financial staff became more anxious about cash flows for 1970 and 1971. They were not anxious about 1969 itself, the existing bank borrowing limit of £70m would be sufficient for immediate needs. But the cash flow forecast made in October 1969 showed that the company would need £20m more than this £70m limit before 1973. Thereafter each successive forecast seemed to show a worse position than the last. The government had been warned of Rolls-Royce's concern over cash and yet in June 1970 Sir Denning told shareholders in the annual report that the board was satisfied that the company had sufficient working capital (later, he admitted to the Inspectors that, in retrospect, the word 'satisfied' was misleading). Indeed another cash flow forecast, made in June 1970, suggested that even if they took up a £20m loan then being considered by the Industrial Reorganization Corporation that would not be enough even for 1970, let alone 1973!

At the annual general meeting in July 1970, Sir Denning told the shareholders that the company was 'in good shape' and he talked about 'reaping the benefits' from the RB 211—the latest estimates showed that the project would make a loss. In October, a new cash flow forecast suggested that £55m would be needed before 1973. Lord Cole now took over as chairman and on 30 October he saw the Prime Minister and soon after the government agreed to a (conditional) loan of £42m. A few days later Lord Cole had obtained an increase in the bank borrowing limit of £18m, to £88m. So, in a few days Lord Cole had apparently conjured up £60m to cover the £55m cash requirement for the next two years.

There were two snags, however. The first concerned the government loan of £42m, for this was conditional upon a satisfactory report on Rolls-Royce's prospects from Cooper Brothers, the accountants, and they could not be expected to complete their study for some months. The second concerned the additional £18m where a ridiculous misunderstanding occurred. The current limit of £70m was provided by overdraft limits of £25m at each of two banks plus £20m acceptances. The new limit was to be provided by £20m overdrafts at these two banks plus new loans totalling £18m. These limits were duly reduced but the loans were not ready, so Rolls-Royce now found itself with a limit of £60m! And now a further problem appeared: when Cooper Bros. saw Rolls-Royce's latest profit forecasts for the following five years they thought they looked too optimistic. Their senior partner, Sir Henry Benson, saw Lord Cole. He agreed. And they agreed on something else too; the extra £60m that Lord Cole had raised to cover the next two years was not going to be enough. £80m was more like it.

On 11 January 1971 a new cash flow forecast suggested that £80m was not enough. £120m was more like it. Each new forecast reflected the new higher R&D costs for the RB 211 and the new lower profit figures for the company as a whole. On 19 January a new estimate showed that they would need that £60m plus another £34m in 1971 *alone*. Lord Cole met Sir Henry again on 20 January and pondered the fearful dilemma of incurring penalties of perhaps £50m if the RB 211 was not delivered on time or perhaps £300m if it was not delivered at all. He wrote to the Ministry of Aviation the next day and on 22 January he, Sir Henry and Mr Morrow (deputy chairman) met at the ministry and then went on to see the governor of the Bank of England, Lord Poole (the chairman of Lazards), and the Westminster Bank. The purpose of all this frantic activity was to draw up the outline of a two-year moratorium under which all the creditors of the company (except very small ones) would be asked not to press their claims for two years and, for their part, Rolls-Royce would undertake to cease all non-essential work and expenditure. The agreement of these banks and the government were necessary, of course, hence that dash round the power points of the City. The Prime Minister was advised of the deteriorating situation on 23 January.

On the 24th, Sunday, Sir Henry and the company's lawyer, Mr Benham, had to confess that they could not devise a moratorium that would work, chiefly because of the unknown size of any claim that Lockheeds might make under the contract. On 25 January Sir Henry had to recommend that a Receiver be appointed. It was the only alternative left to the company. He thought that the government would not be wise to shoulder the burden of the RB 211 although they would probably have to take over those parts of Rolls-Royce that were concerned with defence. The board met on the 26th and after being told of the technical and financial problems were told of the plan to appoint a Receiver. They were stunned.

Not having met since 17 December 1970 they were apparently quite ignorant of the situation.

On 29 January the government took the decision not to support Rolls-Royce any further. Not only would it cost £150m of public money but there was considerable anxiety that, in supporting the company in its dire state, they might be liable at law for participating in the running of a company knowing it was, or could be, insolvent. There was now only a tiny ray of hope in the shape of Mr Dan Houghton, the chief executive of Lockheeds, who was due in Britain on 2 February. Meanwhile Lord Cole was coming to the conclusion that Rolls-Royce might already be insolvent and should cease to trade but, because the Prime Minister was in telephonic communication with Dr Kissinger, the President's assistant, the board agreed to wait. Mr Houghton duly arrived. He was already somewhat concerned over Lockheed's own difficult financial situation and when told of the position of Rolls-Royce he was dazed. He saw bankruptcy for Lockheeds, several sub-contractors and at least two airlines. He said he could almost certainly do nothing to help, certainly not without much more time.

On 3 February the board met, but were asked not to do anything for 24 hours because the President would telephone the Prime Minister that afternoon and Mr Houghton was at Downing Street. Lord Beeching and Sir Maurice Laing (both non-executive directors) tried in vain to persuade the Prime Minister to take over the RB 211 contract rather than allow a company like Rolls-Royce to go into liquidation. The Cabinet met at 4.0 p.m. The President phoned to say he would do what he could to help Lockheed. The cabinet decided to buy parts of Rolls-Royce from the Receiver but to ask him to try to renegotiate the contract with Lockheed.

At 8.30 a.m. on 4 February 1971 the board met, the announcements were made, the Stock Exchange informed and the Receiver appointed.

Expert opinion

The two Inspectors, MacCrindle and Godfrey, have no doubts where to place the blame for the failure of Rolls-Royce. They say that, when considering a project which goes to the foundation of a company's business, no member of the board can stand to one side. The directors, then, are to blame, for they did not ask themselves what might go wrong with this project and what the consequences might then be. But the Inspectors also point out that so highly experienced were Sir Denning and Sir David, and so great was their standing within the board and the company, that the other directors could not fail to lean heavily on their advice. These two men were so convinced that Rolls-Royce must enter this area of business that it coloured their whole approach and in advocating 'this rash commitment' to their colleagues they failed properly to discharge the responsibilities of stewardship.

The Inspectors go on to list a considerable number of causes. First, in setting their sights on developing a big engine and selling it to America, Rolls-Royce had to take several technical steps that were bigger than any they had taken before, in order to catch up with the Americans. But they were not too well placed for this task, having cut back on several R&D facilities, including the RB 178, for example. Second, the company was highly geared in the sixties, having had a bad patch in 1961; it was in no condition to have another.

Third, the terms of the Lockheed contract really were very tough, especially in that prices were virtually fixed. Fourth, even if the launching costs had not risen at all, these were known to be 30 per cent of the company's entire net worth at the time the decision was made. But every engineer knows that estimates of R&D expenditures can be wrong by a factor of 2 or 3 or even 6·5 (according to NASA, RAND, the Downing Report, a Ministry of Supply report, etc.). This should have been 'trite knowledge' to Rolls-Royce, as the Inspectors put it. That the RB 211 might incur a cost equal to the entire net worth of the company was predictable—for all over-spending was to be met, not by the government, not by Lockheed, but by Rolls-Royce alone. Fifth, Sir David was heading the sales effort in America when he should have been providing much needed leadership as head of DED. Sixth, the main board was ignorant of the true situation for much of the time. The Inspectors identify two reasons for this. While strongly rejecting the theory that Rolls-Royce failed because of poor accounting information, they do agree that, as with so many companies, the information system was deficient. In particular, the board were given two documents at each meeting, a green folder and a red folder. The green folder contained all the important matters to be discussed and was compulsory reading for all directors. All the financial data—masses of it in great detail—were in the red folder, i.e., the voluntary one, which few of the directors would have had time to absorb. The other reason was that 'the personalities on the financial side were out-gunned and out-numbered by those on the engineering side'. (For example, in 1969 the DED board had 22 members of whom only one was not an engineer.)

The Inspectors conclude, then, that it was not the Bristol merger that caused Rolls-Royce to fail, nor the costing system, nor the banks, nor Lockheeds, nor the UK government. It was the RB 211 project. It should never have been undertaken. In my opinion this conclusion is correct only as far as it goes and it does not go far enough. In my view, the cause ran wider and deeper; I believe that the strategic decision, 'build a big jet and sell it to the Americans' was the more fundamental error. From it flowed the decision to build the too-ambitious RB 211, the too-tough Lockheed contract, the too-defensive Bristol merger—everything, *including the RB 211 itself*, resulted from that one big decision. It may be asked what alternative strategy Rolls-Royce could have adopted in the early sixties. I do not know, but the Inspectors point out that no alternatives were considered. Does that really mean that there were none, as Sir Denning seems to have believed? (I cannot help thinking that Bristol were on the right track, or at least on a possible alternative track, when they started talking to Pratt and Whitney and Snecma about collaborating on a big engine. Should Rolls-Royce have thought of that back in 1963? Or something else on those lines? Or something?)

Some of the comments in the Press at the time of the Inspectors' report are interesting. The *Financial Times* drew particular attention, in an article of 3 August 1973, to the mistake of putting all your eggs in one basket—especially a speculative one, and especially when the company's finances are not in good shape. But the *Financial Times* was concerned also about the political aspects of the failure. The question that arises is whether a private profit-making company should be asked to undertake a project of national significance unless the government has pledged its full participation. The Inspectors noted this problem but had not been asked to comment on government policy so they kept quiet. The *Financial Times* returned to it later, however, when they note that the same thing happened with the Spey engine a decade earlier—Rolls-Royce spent considerable sums of capital on which the only likely return would be to improve the nation's balance of payments rather than the company's profits. The fact is, said the *Financial Times*, that no one yet has found a practical way by which a government can finance projects in private industry. Some say they should keep out of high technology entirely; others that they should fund it fully; others that the government should take an equity shareholding in the company undertaking the project.

In another article, the *Financial Times* sees a number of lessons that the Inspectors did not emphasize. They note that Rolls-Royce had divisions and profit centres and management services—all the trappings of modern management as recommended in the textbooks. All in vain. The data given to the board was too detailed, the head office was inextricably confused with DED at Derby, divisional boards were rubber stamps, divisional accounts were all on different bases, there was no central financial control. If good financial control and effective corporate planning had been present, Rolls-Royce would never have undertaken the Lockheed contract. (At the time of this article, two years after the crash, Rolls-Royce (1971) still did not have a corporate planning department.)

The *Economist*, in its issue of 4 August 1973, draws attention to the running down of the company's R&D facilities, especially the stress office at Derby. Everything stems, says the *Economist*, from the lack of technical skill to develop an engine like the RB 211. The tough contract was not itself a cause, for if Rolls-Royce had not kept the price as low as they did they would not have landed the contract and would then have gone into decline. Rolls-Royce were wrong to accept a fixed amount of aid from the government and the government were even more at fault for offering it.

Robert Heller, writing in the *Observer*, made several most interesting comments. He thought the Inspectors should have laid more blame on the management (a) for continuing to pay out dividends when the true profits—as opposed to the profits declared—did not cover the dividends (he was referring to the capitalized research costs, of course) and (b) for not ensuring that the company was in a fit financial state before tackling even a sound major project, let alone an unsound one. (To do them justice, the Inspectors are critical of the way Rolls-Royce capitalized those R&D expenditures; and yet one can argue that £10m spent on R&D for a new product is just as much a *capital* investment as £10m spent building a factory for an existing product. This is a matter on which accountants continue to debate with some vigour.) Heller is entitled to be heard with some respect here for back in 1969 he pointed out that Rolls-Royce's profits in 1967 were not fairly reported in the published accounts because of this treatment of R&D expenditure.

Heller further argues that a chief executive should be the servant of his board, not its master. He notes, as others have, that Rolls-Royce had allowed their technical facilities to decline, especially at the Derby stress office, and their legendary skills no longer existed in sufficient measure. He also accuses the Inspectors of failing to understand the rôle of a finance function in a company. The Inspectors said that even if the financial reporting system had worked efficiently it would not have saved the company. I understand Heller to say that it would—someone would have noticed the serious cash position and gone out and done something. Surely Heller is correct: Lord Cole did just that within days of taking over as chairman. But then the criticism being made here is of the lack of response by top management to known financial data, rather than the lack of data. Finally Heller blames the government for entrusting this project to a firm that was neither financially nor managerially fit to undertake it.

Interim conclusions

The purpose of this chapter was to discover how many of the symptoms and causes of failure that we listed in the earlier chapters could be identified in the case of Rolls-Royce. I believe the level of confirmation is remarkably high. I shall consider the salient points first and then briefly list some of the lesser ones.

MANAGEMENT

We were warned of five possible dangers in top management structure and four of them were present in Rolls-Royce:

1. One-man rule. Sir Denning certainly stood head and shoulders above the others on the main board and, as an ironic bonus, Sir David ruled the DED board to a similar extent. So we have that one twice!
2. Unbalanced top team. The Inspectors made particular note of this when they remarked on the preponderance of engineers over accountants.
3. Non-participating board. The Inspectors note how the board depended on Sir Denning's advice and how stunned they were when eventually someone told them their company was insolvent.
4. Weak finance function. In fact, the function as a whole may not have been any worse than that in many companies but its voice was not heard at the top levels which is what we were warned about.
5. Management depth. No: Rolls-Royce did have middle management ability in some abundance, so that fault cannot be confirmed.

ACCOUNTING INFORMATION

We were warned about four faults.

1. No costing data. I think Rolls-Royce did have costing data and did know what the RB 211 would cost—indeed the report is full of such estimates.
2. Budgetary control. They had this too.
3. Cash flow forecast. There were plenty of these.
4. Valuation of assets. I do not think this was a problem.

In the case of Rolls-Royce, then, my strong impression is that their accounting systems were no worse than other companies'. There were plenty of messages but they did not get through to the main board. Middle and senior managers knew what was happening—Mr Metcalfe certainly did—but not the top.

CHANGE

We were warned about not responding to change. I know it is a harsh judgement in an industry where lead times are so long, but I believe Rolls-Royce missed the technological bus *and* the market bus right back in the very early sixties or even the late fifties. The fact is that turnover remained static in money terms and actually fell in real terms over a five-year period (1961–65), and this was a symptom of the fact that they had lost touch with market trends and had fallen behind the Americans in technology. The overall strategy of 'build a big engine and sell it to the Americans' would have been right if adopted in 1960, 1961 or 1962. But by 1965 it was the wrong response.

CREATIVE ACCOUNTING

Accountants will argue for years hence whether a company in Rolls-Royce's position should have capitalized its R&D expenditure. There are no firm rules. Yet by doing so it could be argued that Rolls-Royce's published profits were shown in a somewhat optimistic light.

THE BIG PROJECT

We were warned about this—remember Cork's golden rule? We could hardly have wished for a more vivid confirmation of this phenomenon than the RB 211 project!

OVERTRADING

No. I can see no evidence whatever of this. Turnover did not rise rapidly, certainly not faster than capital employed.

INFLATION

Although the rate of inflation had not reached into the fearful figures of the mid-seventies, cost escalation was already taking its toll in the almost-fixed-price clauses of the contract.

BANK LOANS AND GEARING

There is evidence of an inclination on the part of the banks to excessive generosity towards the ailing Rolls-Royce. In view of the very high level of seniority at which so many of the loans were negotiated it would indeed have been surprising to find anything other than traditional prudence, and yet the banks did increase their lending to Rolls-Royce to £88m only three months before insolvency. Even taking into account the boost to everyone's confidence given by the £42m loan the government had just (conditionally) promised, this was rather remarkable. As to Rolls-Royce's gearing, it was patently high throughout the decade, with interest charges absorbing a significant percentage of profits (except in the three years preceding the merger).

RESCUE

Although Rolls-Royce went broke with considerable impetus a very large proportion of the original company has been resuscitated and is operating profitably.

MANAGERS SEE IT FIRST

There is no evidence in the report to suggest that Sir Denning or Sir David knew of the approaching disaster in 1969 or even in 1970. Nor did the main board—and so no one forced Sir Denning to face the facts—on the contrary the government was encouraging him to drive on. Neither the auditors, nor the banks, nor the customers saw it coming, although evidently the stock market did—the shares started to fall quite sharply relative to the *Financial Times Index* in 1968 when the high hopes of the merger began to fade and this relative decline continued to the end. Middle management may have seen it in 1969—Mr Metcalfe certainly did.

OTHER SYMPTOMS OF FAILURE

We did not have much success with Altman's Z, although, had an observer calculated Z after adjusting the profits for the capitalized R&D they might well have been anxious in 1969. Several other financial ratios looked decidedly weak soon after the merger but they recovered up to 1969 before deteriorating again almost unanimously in 1970. I doubt if any of these financial symptoms could have been relied upon until 1970.

As for non-financial symptoms, there were many. Rolls-Royce did take extended credit from suppliers, there was a lot of cheeseparing (the cancellation of the RB 178 and of a high temperature research engine, the running down of the stress office, etc.). But I am not sure that anyone would have concluded that failure was inevitable from such indications. Furthermore Rolls-Royce did not show many of the other symptoms we were warned about such as poor morale, low pay, poor quality, lack of planning (Rolls-Royce did a lot of planning). No dolly girls either.

Nor did the economic cycle, or a credit squeeze, have any influence. If Altman's analysis is correct, perhaps we should not expect it to, since Rolls-Royce is a big company and relatively immune from credit squeezes. Nor were there any labour troubles.

Two of Dunscombe's comments (see p. 41) are relevant. He explained the importance of a company having a chairman as well as a chief executive. Heller noticed how Sir Denning appeared to be the master of the board rather than its servant and the Inspectors said '... where the main board contained only four non-executive directors to provide a challenge to the executive directors, it was perhaps unfortunate that Sir Denning did not feel able to relinquish the post of chief executive when he succeeded Lord Kindersley as chairman in 1969'. Dunscombe also warned about the growing influence of government in industry and the problem of trying to reconcile the two different sets of objectives that are thus brought together. Let no one underestimate the reality of this. The all too real existence of such a conflict emerged clearly in this case and was the subject of much rather inconclusive comment in the press, as noted on page 92.

6. *Penn Central*

My aim in this chapter is the same as in the last one, to use a well-documented case of failure to verify the interim conclusions of the previous chapters. Here I shall describe the collapse of the Penn Central Transportation Company in the same detail as I described the failure of Rolls-Royce in the last chapter and I shall again rely heavily upon the report of an official government inquiry. This one, 800 pages long and containing hundreds of tables of figures, was published in December 1972 by the US Senate Committee on Commerce. But in this case I shall also be able to draw upon an excellent and very thoroughly researched book called *The Wreck of the Penn Central*, by Daughen and Binzen.

Once again, because this story is a complex one, I shall divide the chapter into sections and again in the last few sections I shall bring together the views of several experts, including Altman, who made comments on the causes and symptoms of this failure. But first I must sketch the preceding 130 years of Penn Central's existence—or, to be accurate, of Penn Central's antecedent's existence. Penn Central itself only lived for 872 days from the day of the merger (which made it the sixth largest company

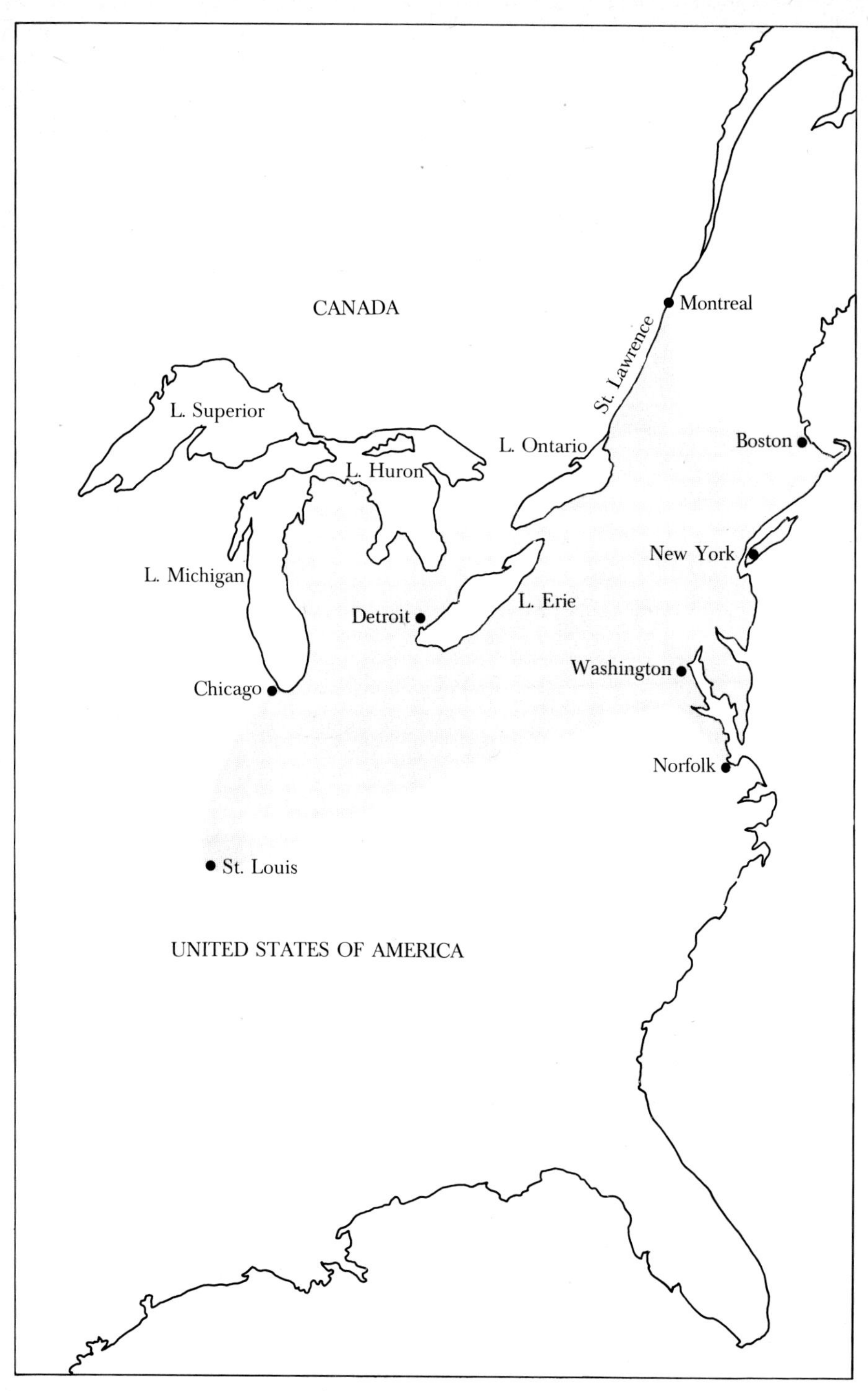

Exhibit 6.1. Sketch map of the eastern part of North America showing area served by Penn Central

in America) to 21 June 1970 when it filed its petition. But that is the end of the story; let me start at the beginning.

Penn Central's pedigree

The story begins in the early nineteenth century, when the railroad barons punched their way across the United States. Punched may even be an understatement, for competition was not gentlemanly at the time that the Pennsylvania Railroad (PRR) and New York Central (NYC) were born. The relationship between these two was particularly acrimonious because they both served the same enormous industrialized area in the north-east of the country (see Exhibit 6.1). They were both extremely successful—they were the number one and number two railroads in the USA—and both extremely powerful. Competition between them became so suicidal that, in 1885, John Pierpoint Morgan, the banker, brought the two bosses together and made them agree to reduce the level of competition. This was quite an achievement, for the two companies were then (and remained) very different in character. PRR was managed by professional, upper-middle-class, conventional, dull and honest men. But NYC was a child of Cornelius Vanderbilt who, to put it politely, was a wheeler-dealer. His colourful financial techniques had made him the richest man in America.

But now that they were carving up the market in their own interests instead of cutting each other's throats, the power of both companies increased still further. The government responded by setting up the Interstate Commerce Commission (ICC) in 1887 to supervise the behaviour of railroads. The response of PRR and NYC was to grow even larger by merger and acquisition. In fact, the whole railroad system in America expanded and boomed for several decades until some time around the turn of the century when events began to move against them. In 1916, for example, the government took over the whole railroad system and ran it until the end of the war—by which time the track and the other physical assets had become badly run down. In an attempt to revitalize the industry, the ICC was given powers under the 1920 Transportation Act to arrange railroad mergers—an insult that prompted PRR and NYC to arrange a number of their own mergers rather than any proposed by ICC.

The depression of the thirties saw PRR still paying a dividend while most other railroads, including NYC, were either on the brink of bankruptcy or actually over it. It was a current joke that one third of all the track in the USA was operated by Receivers. And yet the thirties saw a remarkable number of railroad innovations, including streamlining, diesels and electrification. Perhaps the stimulus behind this was the clear indication that motor vehicles were beginning to eat into freight and passenger services alike. But that was only one symptom; the whole character of the economy was changing; it was changing rapidly and it was all going in one direction—away from the railways. Some concrete examples will illustrate what was happening all through the middle decades of this century.

Take coal, for example. Everyone knows that carrying coal is a major part of a railway's work load. And yet during these decades it gradually became less economic to take coal by rail to power stations sited near the user—far better to build the power station near the coal and transmit the electricity. For this reason among others, coal, which gave the railways 29 per cent of their business in 1950, gave them 17 per cent in 1960 and 15 per cent in 1970. But for PRR and NYC a second blow was that the coal in their area of USA gradually became less popular because of its high sulphur content. Nor was it only coal that was in decline; railways were built when steel, corn, minerals and other primary goods were all-important. Gradually, as the US economy developed, these primary goods declined relative to high-value goods and services. (Services, for example, formed only nine per cent of US GNP in 1950 but 13 per cent by 1970.) So intercity freight carried by all means of transport rose by only 43 per cent in a decade which saw GNP rise by 49 per cent.

The share of this intercity traffic carried by rail declined. A lot of freight began to go down the new interstate highways in large fast container lorries direct from door to door, which rail could no longer do—new industries had appeared quite suddenly in places miles from any track. High-value freight began to go by air—so did people, of course. The St Lawrence Seaway was opened in the late fifties, thus obviating the need to transfer freight from ship to rail on the way to and from the great industries around Lake Ontario. Pipelines were laid and took yet more bulk materials away from rail. In the two decades from 1950 the railroad's share of the total freight market fell from 56 to 40 per cent.

As a result of all these trends and changes, most railroads were in continuous financial difficulty. Certainly PRR and NYC were. Of course, the railroads fought their competitors by fair means *and* foul (see Daughen and Binzen, for example, on how a court case brought by lorry operators against the railroads was enlivened by the appearance of a Miss Sonya Saroyan).

Gradually it became clear to many observers that a major reorganization of the north-eastern railroad system was needed. In particular, the chairman of PRR, J. M. Symes, formed the strong personal opinion that a merger of PRR and NYC was now the right solution for all concerned.

The merger talks

Discussions between the two companies began in September 1957. Symes of PRR met Young and Perlman of NYC, but only a few months later Young shot himself and Perlman took over the company, thus becoming a key figure in the story. Alfred E. Perlman had joined NYC only three years previously, as deputy to Young, with a very high reputation within the industry. His claim to fame was that he had been appointed to head a small railroad company which had gone bankrupt four times and had paid no dividends for 76 years. Within a year he had 'turned it round'.

Unfortunately, while Perlman agreed in principle that this merger—the biggest ever contemplated in USA—was necessary, he did not like Symes. The companies did not much like each other either—their styles were quite different. And although nearly equal in size, they were not equal in power. For one thing, PRR owned a substantial share in the Norfolk & Western Railway and the reason that this was such a weighty bargaining counter was that Norfolk & Western was itself quite large and actually made a handsome profit! Perlman felt that Symes would have the upper hand and that the merger would be 'unbalanced'. He broke off the talks in 1959.

Perlman had realized that mergers in the industry were now inevitable, so he went off to talk to two other railroads popularly known as the B & O and the C & O. They were not interested for the very good reason that they were to announce their own merger a few months later. Perlman was now worried. Ranged against his NYC in the east were not only PRR but the proposed B & O and C & O merger and later, no doubt, a number of other new groupings. In a desperate attempt to thwart the B & O and C & O merger he bought 20 per cent of B & O shares. He also appealed to the ICC to allow him to join another proposed grouping, the Norfolk & Western—Nickel Plate—Warbash. I believe it can be said that Perlman had not really thought out what alternative there was to the PRR merger until after he had broken off the talks; I also believe that Symes had outmanoeuvred Perlman. Nor is this surprising, for while Perlman was essentially a railroad operator, Symes, like so many of his predecessors at PRR, was a political operator. There was something else that Perlman should have known; the Transportation Act of 1940 had, in effect, given PRR virtual right of veto on any railroad merger in the north-east.

So Perlman now (1961) went back to Symes to reopen talks on a merger, but this time PRR was clearly going to be senior partner in the merged company. In brief, the idea now was that PRR would divest itself of its holding in Norfolk & Western (which would join up with several other railroads) and NYC would divest itself of its holding in B & O (which would join up with another grouping). Symes and Perlman quickly reached agreement, their boards agreed in January 1962 and the shareholders agreed in May.

A slight hitch

A merger between PRR and NYC had been the subject of discussion in public, in the two companies, in ICC, in several state and federal agencies and in the White House for five years. One would have thought, then, that once the shareholders had agreed, the whole matter would have been completed within a few months. But we must not forget that a railroad company is a common carrier and has a duty to the public (it was Cornelius Vanderbilt's son who in a similar context made the immortal remark, 'The Public be damned'). Railroad companies cannot even close a branch line without a thorough investigation to ensure that it is not against the public interest. There are trade unions, too, who must look after the interests of the employees, especially when there are going to be 120 000 of them. There are other railroads in the area whose business must not be damaged by the merger. There are customers and suppliers of the railroads. Every town and village could be threatened by the use of the monopoly power created by such a merger—the combined turnover of PRR and NYC exceeded $1·5bn in 1962.

Let us not forget that ICC had not only this merger before it but the ones involving B & O and C & O were still under consideration, as was one concerning Norfolk & Western. All over the USA other railroad mergers were being proposed and it occurred to President Kennedy that it was time to examine the whole question of mergers and the public interest. So he set up the Interagency Committee on Transport Mergers to lay down policy guidelines. I think it is fair to say that at that time no one knew how to strike a balance between the public and private interests. (It is equally fair to say that the Interagency Committee did not resolve this paradox and that it remains unresolved to this day.)

In December 1962 the ICC approved the merger of B & O and C & O and was roundly criticized for making this decision in isolation from the other merger proposals before it. Meanwhile 200 trade unions, state agencies, trade associations, railroad companies and members of the public began putting their objections to the ICC concerning the proposed PRR–NYC merger (which I shall now call the PC merger).

The hearings ended in favour of the merger in October 1963. Then the process of appeals against that decision began. At that time Symes, who years ago had started the whole thing, now retired to be replaced as head of PRR by Stuart T. Saunders. Saunders had been chairman of Norfolk & Western and must take some of the credit for its excellent record. He certainly had a very high reputation and was, as one would expect of a PRR director, a man of accomplishments and good connections. But on the very day he was appointed, the Interagency Committee on Mergers, having set out policy guidelines for mergers in general, announced its opposition to the PC merger in particular.

It should be noted that 18 months had now elapsed since the shareholders gave their approval to the merger. One of the merger terms was that 1·0 PRR share would be considered equal to 1·3 NYC shares which was a fair valuation in May 1962. The companies were still operating independently, however, and it was so far pure luck that this ratio was still valid after 18 months.

One of the railroads which had not been invited to join any of these mergers was the New Haven. It applied to join the PC merger but ICC refused the request, commenting 'it would impose a persistent and substantial burden . . .'. The debate rumbled on. 1963 went, so did 1964 and 1965. Saunders and Perlman struggled nobly not only to keep their respective companies afloat but to overcome the countless objections raised by unions and agencies and commissions and associations . . . 1966, 1967. Finally the Interagency Committee on Mergers agreed to withdraw its objections if the decrepit New Haven company was allowed to join the merger. The High Court enforced this decision and the merger was at last approved. One cannot help asking what it was about the inclusion of this awful little railroad that swung the Interagency Committee round to approve the PC merger. The answer, according to the Senate Committee Report, is that the government failed to face up to the problems of the railroads—New Haven being a typical casualty—and it was a case of 'sweeping the problem of New Haven under the Penn Central rug'.

The merger was approved at last, then, and it officially took place at one minute past midnight on 1 February 1968—six years after the shareholders had agreed the terms and over a decade since the talks first began.

'Imaginative accounting'

During the whole of this period, PRR and NYC, along with most other railroad companies, had their ups and downs. Mainly downs. Taking the two companies together they made a total profit of $380m on their railroad operations during the six-year merger period 1962–67. Against this were fixed interest charges on loans of $475m, so it was just as well that both companies had non-rail income of $350m during that period. Even so, this only gave an overall profit before tax for six years of $250m which is not excessive compared with dividends paid out totalling $200m and capital expenditure of $1200m.

One does not have to be a top-grade accountant to see that this does not look too good—unless there is ample borrowing capacity of course. But the combined equity of these two companies in those years was worth approximately $2300m and long-term debts alone was already at £1200m at the start of this six-year period. Who is going to lend to a company earning around $40m a year on $2300m equity—less than two per cent? In fact, quite a number of people must have, because their long-term debt nearly reached $2000m by 1970!

Not only were the results looking very poor but both companies, while still operating separately, somehow had to preserve the 1·0 to 1·3 ratio of profits and dividends during the whole of this six-year period after the terms had been agreed. In order to do this and also to buttress their credit ratings, both companies engaged in some interesting accounting techniques. NYC really only used two. They were able to maintain their dividend payments, and even increase them, by simply borrowing the necessary cash; and, second, they made extensive use of equipment and vehicle leasing to reduce the apparent gearing (this was, incidently, also done to circumvent one of the merger terms on debt limitation). PRR also engaged in extensive leasing for the same reasons but they developed a comprehensive, sustained and ingenious campaign of distortion, led, it appears, by Saunders but captained in the field and technically directed by the PRR finance man, David C. Bevan. The campaign was called 'profit maximization' and my chapter sub-title comes from a memo that Bevan once wrote commending one of his staff for what he called his 'imaginative accounting'. I will describe only some of the techniques.

First, they cut expenditure on the track itself because, for a reason peculiar to US railroads, nearly all such expenditure has to be treated as an expense when made (whereas by almost all other accounting definitions it would be capital). Second, they began to capitalize major overhaul expenditure, a practice specifically condemned by ICC and, in fact, by most accountants. Third, all subsidiary companies were asked to treat extraordinary income as ordinary and vice versa with their expenses. Fourth, some of the 'earnings' from some of the subsidiaries during this time were found later, after the merger of course, to be nothing more than paper profits on property deals. Fifth, in the 1964 accounts the earnings from 41 subsidiaries were included in PRR's consolidated profits. In the 1965 accounts the earnings from 100 subsidiaries were shown. The technique was to reduce the qualification for inclusion from 100 per cent owned subsidiaries to 50 per cent owned.

The campaign achieved its objectives, and not only were the two companies still afloat six years after the agreement, but were still apparently lying in the ratio 1·0 to 1·3. It was quite an impressive achievement. It had one unfortunate side-effect. When PC eventually collapsed it probably did so with more violence than it would have done if this profit maximization policy had not been instituted.

The merger

One of the arguments that Saunders and Perlman put up to the ICC in favour of the merger was that it would result in substantial savings. A figure of $100m per annum was mentioned. Whether this sum would ever have been achieved no one now can say, but PC's records do suggest that $64m was saved. Against those savings there were, unfortunately, costs of $250m, making a net cash outflow due to the merger of nearly $190m during the two years of PC's existence. Three things went wrong.

First, there was the inclusion of the New Haven Railroad which, as predicted by everyone, was a drain on PC's resources. It cost $30m in the two years (and it also received a loan from PC of $14m). Second, PC had to pay redundancy and other payments to employees and, at trade union insistence, took back into employment 5000 people dismissed as redundant in previous years. This caused a cash flow of $60m in the two years.

Third, there were operational problems which cost $30m and alterations to equipment which cost $90m. Both of these categories of cost were due to PC's decision to carry out the physical merging of the two companies' track, not in four years as had been planned, but in two. The idea of accelerating the programme was to achieve the urgently needed savings as soon as possible, but the financial effect of this haste was merely to accelerate the drain on cash flows while the physical effects were chaotic. Although it is true that a number of freight terminals, shunting yards, track interconnections and so on were smoothly and efficiently built or rebuilt, service was severely disrupted. They did not only lose a few trucks or rail-vans in the *mêlée*—whole trains disappeared! So did a lot of irate customers. Some of the customers who still did business with them did not pay because the two companies' computer systems were not compatible and they were not sent their bills.

Nor was the chaos limited to the railroad itself. The accounting and costing systems were different. The marketing philosophy, the attitude to employees, the employees themselves, were all different and, in the time now allowed for the merger to take place, quite incompatible.

Finally, as luck would have it, the economy began to turn down quite sharply, and railroads are, and always have been, one of the industries that are quite severely affected by economic conditions. The fact that fixed assets form such a large proportion of the total cost of running a railroad makes it particularly sensititive to changes in the volume of business.

The last few months

All through 1968 and 1969 the economy continued to decline. Rail services worsened; although many passengers thought they could not do so any further, they did. An appalling winter added to the burdens of the ailing company in 1970. Points froze solid and power lines snapped in the cold. The trains were noisy, dirty, uncomfortable, cold, late and sometimes dangerous. They always had been but now it grew worse and worse.

Parallel with this was the fact that PC was desperately short of cash; they always had been, but now this also grew worse and worse. There were a number of reasons for this. One of the reasons was that when PRR had sold its shares in Norfolk & Western for $300m they had reinvested almost the whole of it in property thus perpetuating the cash shortage that both companies had experienced for years. A golden opportunity to raise cash had also been missed at the time of the merger itself for at the time there was considerable public optimism for, and interest in, the merger and an equity issue or a debenture would surely have been well subscribed. Also, as we have seen, the merger itself cost $250m in two years instead of less than half that over four. Yet another reason was that PC made a loss in 1969 of $83m and in 1970 of $326m (and we cannot be too sure of these figures, for the profit maximization policy was in operation; one guess is that the 1969 loss was understated by $46m).

A further reason for the cash shortage was that PC was owed approximately $50m by other railroad companies. All the track of the railroad companies is physically interconnected, of course, with countless daily traffic movements across company boundaries. By a complex system agreed between them, one company would bill the customer and split the income with any other company who had handled the consignment. It was their share of these just dues that PC now became so slow to collect. For these many and varied reasons PC was desperately short of cash. In 1968 they were already having to rely heavily on Eurodollars, revolving bank credit, commercial paper and debt offerings. In the summer the revolving bank credit reached its $100m limit but was renewed and extended to $300m by First National City Bank of New York who, however, asked for strict maintenance of offsetting bank balances.

Late in 1968, PC obtained permission from ICC for $100m commercial paper issues which were sold late in 1968. Another $50m was sold in March 1969. In the spring, PC tried to raise a $200–300m mortgage on its very considerable properties but no one was willing to take them up. So PC went back to ICC for another $50m issue, permission for which was granted although ICC was not happy about these issues. Normally commercial paper is for 270 days but in this case it was for a whole year. In any case, said ICC severely, it is not good practice to use such short-term money for capital projects or for refinancing maturing long-term debts but, as PC 'was in a strong financial condition' and as it was going out for some long-term finance as soon as possible, ICC allowed the issue. (I have no idea from where this long-term finance might have come—we have seen what had just happened to their mortgage offer!)

By late 1969, ICC had heard from both official and unofficial sources that PC was in difficulties. But they appear only, or chiefly, to have been aware of the operating difficulties on the railroad itself, not with the financial problems. On 27 January the banks lent PC another $50m in revolving credit, 'to proceed with its orderly financing program', although this time there were strings attached. In March (during that terrible winter when, incidently, losses were running at $1m per day) Bevan, the finance director, prepared a document for the banks as background for a new loan for $100m he was asking for. Before it could be printed PC's results for the first quarter were published (on 22 April) showing a loss of $62m. PC's shares dropped sharply. The loan prospectus was withdrawn for rewriting and reissuing—it was absolutely essential that money be raised soon, for not only did PC have to finance the losses now being made, but there was no less than $78m of loans maturing between 21 April and 22 May.

Meanwhile Saunders arranged to meet John Volpe, the Secretary of the Department of Transportation, in an effort to persuade him to urge President Nixon's administration to nationalize PC's passenger service or to do something, anything, to help PC in what was fast becoming a crisis.

On 12 May the loan prospectus reappeared but failed to impress the bankers. Confidence had gone. Out of the 25 directors on PC's board, 16 were bankers, yet no one came forward with a short-term loan and certainly not a long one, not unless the government gave its guarantee. Saunders saw Volpe again but when PC was asked for a cash flow forecast there was none available. On 15 May a stockbroker, hitherto well known for always putting his clients into PC, started to sell for them. The shares fell to $10 (from $86 two years before). Standard and Poor de-rated the shares to 'speculative'. On 21 May, Bevan had to admit that the $100m loan issue was a failure and the prospectus was withdrawn. On 1 June he went to First National City Bank, the leading bank in the PC story, but got nothing. He got nothing again on the third and fourth. One reason for this lack of success was that the head of this bank, Walter

Wriston, was about to ask Saunders to let Bevan go. On 8 June both Bevan and Saunders left the company. Gorman took over and the shares rose to $13.25.

On 9 June the government began seriously to consider how to save the company. Perhaps the Navy, with its large transport requirements would put up some money? Or the Defense Department? Half a dozen Senate Committees sat and discussed making a loan of $200m, or one of $750m or not making any loans at all. On 19 June the Defense Department decided not to guarantee a loan and the President concurred.

On 21 June 1970 the board met and filed a petition for reorganization under Section 77 of the Bankruptcy Act. This procedure allowed the Receiver to continue to run the railway almost indefinitely.

The Senate Committee's opinion

In their conclusions, the Senate Committee draw attention to the hostile environment in which PC had to operate where competition was immense and profits were too low to allow survival. They recognized the decline of coal, especially high sulphur coal, as one major element in this environment, the sluggish and cyclical US economy as another, the government-assisted highways and seaways, airways and pipelines as another.

But that does not mean the management were not at fault—far from it. PRR should not have put their cash into property, it should have been available for the railroad; they should not have used those profit maximization techniques; they should not have merged with NYC; neither company should have paid dividends from such low profits; Saunders and Bevan should have obtained more cash at the time of the merger; they should all have followed market trends more closely; they should not have agreed to the New Haven joining the merger nor to pay out all that money for labour; they should have cooperated more closely after the merger; they should not have made such wasteful haste after the merger; and so on and so on.

The Committee also blames the other railroads, in particular for the way they invariably looked after their own individual interests. Could they not just occasionally have risen above this parochial view and proposed industry-wide schemes? Such as one for improving the way small loads were handled between them, for example.

The Committee then turn their attention to the rôle of government and its various agents in this affair. Congress, it says, has always held aloof from these problems because of its policy of not interfering with private industry except when it was necessary to protect the public and the customers. The Senate Committee believed the time had come for Congress to consider more carefully the relationship between government and railroads. Equally, it was clear that the executive branches of government had failed to work out what their basic attitude should be. Thus, for example, either the Administration was against the merger—and it certainly said it was against it in the ICC hearings—for good reasons or for trivial ones. If they were good reasons, why did the eventual agreement of Saunders and Perlman to the inclusion of New Haven overcome them? (I ought to add, without knowing whether it is significant, that meanwhile two changes of President had occurred.) As for the Department of Transportation, it seems not to have been aware of PC's problems until two or three weeks before their petition was announced. In general, the Committee believe that the government was so busy papering over the cracks in its policy towards the railroads in particular and transport in general that it did not have time to tackle—or even to consider—the real basic problems.

The Committee employs some almost intemperate language over the record of the Interstate Commerce Commission (ICC)—'a docket of dismal failure', it calls it. The ICC was specifically charged with supervising the rail industry in the interests of the public. But it did not analyse problems, it did not propose solutions, it failed to use its authority, it did not monitor the merger, it did not draw attention to PC's extravagant dividends, it did not alert the government when PC was in trouble, it tackled the three sets of merger proposals singly instead of as a whole, and so on.

The Senate Committee go on to make several recommendations. It asks for more disclosure of information by railroad companies in order to make the use of imaginative accounting more difficult. It suggests that companies should prepare cash flow forecasts for a year ahead in order to avoid sudden and unexpected liquidity crises. It recommends that the government should work out a coherent policy towards the railroads, towards transportation and, indeed, towards all private companies providing a public service of any sort. At no time in the whole PC affair, says the Committee, did the government make a single constructive suggestion.

If I can presume to summarize this enormously long and excessively detailed and fragmented report, I would sum up as follows. The PC (and antecedent) management was just not good enough bearing in mind the conditions; in particular Saunders and Bevan should not have gone in for 'profit maximization'. The merger was ill-conceived (the report uses the words 'shotgun marriage') because both companies were virtually bankrupt even before the strain of the merger was imposed upon them—again the managers were partly at fault for pushing it through. The whole story might have been very different if the government and its various agents, particularly that terrible ICC, had worked out a coherent attitude to the railroads. Finally, the Committee feels that the environment was so hostile to PC that it would have taken quite exceptionally good management to extricate it from its troubles.

It would be wrong to say that Daughen and Binzen come to opposite conclusions from the Senate Committee's but they certainly come to different ones.

Daughen and Binzen's opinion

While the Senate Committee fully acknowledge that PC's management made mistakes in plenty, it avoids placing upon them the whole blame for the crash. Daughen and Binzen, on the other hand, come very near to placing the whole burden on three men: Saunders, Bevan and Perlman. In their *Wreck of the Penn Central* they say, 'The railroad's three top officers scarcely spoke to one another. They could not or would not work together . . . each tried to blame the other two.' Now this book is full of facts, figures, quotations and even anecdotes. I am not certain that, in view of the depth of research that the authors put into their study, we may place much less credence on their judgement than on that of the Committee. I shall try to summarize what they say about these three men in the following paragraphs in which, it will be observed, a great deal of information is given that did not appear in the Senate Committee Report.

Let us first consider Saunders. He was a member of several exclusive clubs, he boasted among his friends Walter Annenberg and President Johnson. He was a director of US Steel, Chase Manhattan Bank and Bell Telephones. He was 'Businessman of the Year' in 1968. He did extremely well at Norfolk & Western. So it must have seemed completely appropriate that he should become chief executive of PRR at the age of 54. But, say Daughen and Binzen, he seems to have had it fixed firmly in his mind that his job was, above everything else, to bring about the merger initiated by Symes, his predecessor. He tackled this job with verve and ability and, in the teeth of fierce opposition, with success. But he never once stopped, in all those years, to ask himself whether the merger still made any sense.

Daughen and Binzen interviewed Saunders a few months after the failure and he was still convinced that it was right in principle as would, in time, be demonstrated. His analysis of the causes of the failure are most instructive. In 1945 railroads had something approaching a monopoly of intercity freight—67 per cent, in fact. They were treated as a monopoly then and have been ever since even though their share is now down to 40 per cent. The US government spends billions of dollars each year on roads, billions on aircraft, billions on airports. The railroads get nothing. So the crash was caused by the government not doing anything to help over a period of years and years even though everyone knows that a return on capital of one per cent spells eventual disaster. One cannot even maintain a railroad on that, let alone re-equip it. It was not the merger that caused the crash, said Saunders, not the diversification into property, not New Haven, not the generous deal with the unions, not the recession in the US economy, nor inflation of costs, nor the rise in interest rates. It was all these things heaped upon an industry that was dying because the government had given billions to all the other forms of transportation and nothing to the railroads at all.

Before turning to Perlman we should note that Saunders' rôle in PRR and PC was (in addition to his efforts to push the merger through) mainly that of a high-level contact man with very senior civil servants, bankers, customers and so on. He played a relatively small executive rôle and delegated huge areas of day-to-day operations to subordinates. In particular he delegated the whole of the railroad operations to Perlman and the financial, property and diversification programme to Bevan. Unfortunately, relations between the three men were not good.

Perlman was a highly successful railroad operator but he did not join exclusive clubs and he was a Jew—something very rare in top railroad management circles. As we have seen, he eventually came to recognize that it was not to be a merger of equals and that PRR, not his NYC, would be top dog. What is more, Perlman's boss was Saunders, a PRR man; his most important subordinates were PRR men, too. So if they did not like what Perlman asked them to do they could, he felt, go over his head to Saunders. He did not like Bevan. Bevan kept telling Saunders that Perlman was overspending and that the return on capital invested in Perlman's railroad operations was far too low. Eventually, in December 1969, almost at the end of the PC story, he was 'kicked upstairs' by Saunders and Gorman took over from him.

Perlman's list of causes of the failure, as told to Daughen and Binzen, include the same point that Saunders made about the grossly uneven way in which the government had for years treated the various means of transport in America. He also points to the ridiculous demand that 5000 former employees be uselessly re-employed, and to the inclusion of the New Haven. But, more important he thought, was the economic recession, cost inflation, high interest rates and the fact that the US post office transferred an enormous volume of mail from rail to air and road. He also believed that his hands were tied by Saunders and Bevan although he did not think that the amounts of money diverted from rail investment to non-rail was so great as to starve the railroad really significantly. (The same point is made by the Senate Committee who note that from 1963–69 only five per cent of all capital expenditure went to non-rail investments.)

Professor Altman's opinion

Altman draws attention to a number of important features in the PC failure. In the first place, the whole railroad system in the USA is a government regulated cartel. That means that its freedom of action to respond to change is heavily qualified. It cannot meet competition by adjusting prices, it cannot close down lines, and its manning levels are rigid. This is on top of the normal railroad rigidity resulting from the simple fact that once a track is laid it cannot easily be moved elsewhere. In addition there was some union featherbedding resulting in a rigid cost structure—a feature of some importance when labour costs are 66 per cent of total operating costs as PC's were (many other railroads were lower, the average being 58 per cent).

Second, there was a shortage of cash caused in part by a poorly managed finance function—he notes how PC continued to pay extravagant dividends and to use cash for buying property. Third, there was the economic cycle. A downturn in the economy together with a decision by President Nixon to use monetary means of economic regulation plus the above-mentioned rigidities and cash shortage could hardly have failed to cause PC immense damage. It would have damaged any company with high fixed costs and high gearing, but railroads are particularly prone to economic depression; two thirds of railroad failures since the Second World War have occurred during months of recession. Recession has occurred in one fifth of all the months since the war. That means that two-thirds of all railroad failures have occurred in one-fifth of the months! Incidently there have been 1100 railroad failures in just under 100 years.

Fourth, the merger. The merger failed, bringing the companies down with it, because it took so long to negotiate, because the expected savings never materialized and because of those costly settlements with labour unions and the New Haven.

Incidentally, Altman notes how the share price of PC fell from \$68 in 1968 to \$43¼ by September 1969. Then from September 1969 to 1 April 1970 they fell to \$23½ while 1½ million shares changed hands. From 1 April to 19 June 1970 (the day before the bankruptcy announcement) they fell to \$11⅛ with five million shares involved.

Another point that Altman makes is that a number of 'sophisticated investors were caught with their wallets exposed' when PC announced its petition. As late as January 1970 the banks were still lending to PC. But it was not only the banks who failed to anticipate the disaster. Everyone who heard the news was stunned. Why? Could it not have been predicted? Professor Murray says it could have been because, from 1965 to 1969 the vital railroad ratio known as net operating income (before tax) divided by gross revenue dropped from around 6·0 to minus 5·0 while other railroads were showing a fall from around 12 to around 6. But, says Altman, although that is quite correct and many people did observe this at the time, this is only one ratio. It happens also to be true that in the same period another vital ratio (total debt/total assets) looked better than the other railroads. It is no good looking at individual ratios, says Altman, you have to develop a comprehensive model on the lines of the one in chapter 4. In a later article Altman actually built a railroad bankruptcy prediction model and shows that PC was a strong candidate as early as 1968.

Interim conclusions

I hope that enough of the PC failure has now been revealed, and a sufficient volume of expert comment has been described, to enable us to draw up a list of interim conclusions. As in the case of Rolls-Royce, so in the case of Penn Central, many of the warnings we were given by the writers and experts have again proved to be valid. I believe a consensus is beginning to form and most of the causes and symptoms of the PC failure can be considered under the following, now familiar, headings.

MANAGEMENT

We can certainly see one of the causes that we were warned about: the board did not participate. Only right at the end—a matter of weeks from bankruptcy—did the board realize what was happening (and 16 out of 25 directors were bankers). We can also claim that the finance function was weak; Bevan was not on the main board. But I do not think that Saunders exercised 'one-man rule'. There is a fairly strong contrary opinion, namely that he delegated far too generously to Bevan and Perlman and did not adequately supervise them. Nor was the top team especially unbalanced. Nor was there a lack of management depth. But there was no separate chairman as distinct from a chief executive. Saunders was both at once.

ACCOUNTANCY INFORMATION

This was certainly lacking. When a cash flow forecast was called for, none was available. The costing systems of PRR and NYC were not compatible—although, in defence of PC is must be assumed that they would have been rendered compatible in time. As to valuation of assets, I am not sure that this caused any problem other than when assets were deliberately over-valued in the profit maximization policy.

CHANGE

No question about this one. PC did not respond to the changes that took place over the last few decades. But the important question is why did PC not respond, for the managers must have known perfectly well what these changes were. I believe they did try to make the necessary responses and that this is precisely what the ill-fated profit maximization policy was all about. What Saunders and Bevan were trying to do, surely, was to move resources out of railroads into more profitable investments such as property and aviation. It failed before it began, not because of poor management (although that may have contributed) but because of the constraints.

CONSTRAINTS

The number of restrictions imposed upon PC before and at the merger were legion. They could not increase fares or close branch lines, they could not reduce manning levels, they could not invest in airlines, their competitors in road, sea and air were subsidized, the merger was held up for six years, they had to accept a derelict partner, they had to take back 5000 employees. . . .

The sources of these constraints were unions, courts, government agencies, pressure groups, public opinion—all the bodies and anti-bodies that now constrain the freedom of companies to make profits in any way they choose. Most businessmen now accept the right of society to regulate their behaviour but it can be argued that in this case the constraints imposed were either excessive or mutually contradictory. It was absurdly contradictory for the government to approve the merger through ICC but disapprove through the Interagency Committee. It was contradictory to expect a profit-making organization to provide a service to the community and subsidize it out of its own profits. My impression, judging from the interviews that Daughen and Binzen had with Saunders and Perlman, is that they had both become exasperated by the inconsistencies of governmental interference—a fact more soberly described and reflected throughout the Senate Committee Report.

ECONOMIC CYCLE

There is little doubt that railroads are severely affected by recessions. The downturn in 1968–70 together with a credit squeeze plus the rising rate of cost inflation substantially worsened PC's plight.

OVERTRADING

No. I can see no sign whatever of this. Turnover was almost static for the last two decades. Capital, that is equity plus loans, increased faster than turnover, so the opposite of overtrading occurred.

BIG PROJECT

Yes. Surely the merger was looked upon by both companies as the one major step that would, in a single blow, lift them off the plateau and solve all their problems. It went wrong in exactly the way the experts described; costs were underestimated, revenues and profits overestimated and the time to bring it to fruition also underestimated.

CREATIVE ACCOUNTING

It is remarkable, bearing in mind that PC was America's sixth largest company, that so little was heard from auditors, bankers, the institutions, the Press, ICC, or anyone else about the 'profit maximization' policy.

BANKS AND GEARING

PC's gearing was excessively high, and so was that of PRR and NYC, throughout most of the sixties. In fact both companies had reduced their gearing, as an act of conscious policy, in the early years of the sixties following its rise due to re-equipping after the war. PRR got theirs down to 0·4 (Long-term debt to equity) by 1964 and NYC to 0·7. But it rose to 0·8 at the merger and thereafter went on rising to 1·27. (Actually it was higher even than that; leasing was used as a deliberate means of reducing apparent gearing.)

The banks seemed quite content to go on financing PC until the bitter end. Why? In addition to the reasons suggested by the experts (see p. 32) there was another in this case (and perhaps in the case of Rolls-Royce also). Many of the PC directors were bankers—14 banks were represented there by the 16 directors. The disadvantages of such 'interlocks' among directorships are fairly obvious. (One of these directors was also chairman of a company that was a PC customer—would he want freight rates to go up or down?)

THE LAST FEW MONTHS

At least four of the phenomena that we are now beginning to associate with the last stages of collapse were visible in this case. The continued generosity of the banks up to a few weeks before insolvency. Then the frantic, even lunatic, scramble to scrape up some cash accompanied by, and parallel with, a marked deterioration of operating efficiencies. Finally the dazed astonishment of everyone—including the board, the stock market, the banks, the auditors, the government, and so on—when the announcement is made.

MANAGERS SEE IT FIRST

I do not think there is any doubt that Saunders and Bevan knew that PRR was doomed about a decade before the failure. That is why they tried so hard to diversify. Bevan sold his shares early in 1969. PC's shares moved down from 1968. I believe that Perlman, however, remained convinced that all that was needed to save the railroad he so plainly cared for was more investment. But I am also sure that none of these three realized just how bad things were until a few weeks before the failure. Bevan says he was 'stunned' to receive the appalling actual versus budget figures in mid-April for the first quarter's operations. By late April, Walter Wriston, chief executive of PC's main bank, began trying to wake up the six PC directors who formed the finance committee.

NON-FINANCIAL SYMPTOMS

There were a number of these—even including a few dolly girls, so sadly lacking in the Rolls-Royce case! More seriously, the operations of PC declined into almost utter chaos as failure approached, there was a long history of cheeseparing, morale was low, customers (especially commuters and other passengers) could hardly fail to notice the declining quality of service, and so on.

RESCUE

No onc will ever know, presumably, whether PC has a profitable core as the experts claim most bankrupt companies have, because the government will ensure that PC goes on, under Section 77 of the Bankruptcy Act, providing a service for the community whether it is profitable to do so or not.

7. *Causes and symptoms*

I have now presented a synopsis of the views of a considerable number of writers and experts in this field, have reproduced several of the lists of causes and symptoms that some of them have published, have briefly described a number of cases of failure and have described in great detail two of the most important failures in recent history. Now in this chapter I want to bring all this together. In itself this is quite a useful thing to do because no one seems ever before to have tried to coordinate all the knowledge about failure that lies scattered through the literature and in the minds of innumerable experts all over the world. Always before each of these lists has been the product of only one man's experience; the list I want to present in this chapter is an amalgam of them all—a list of lists.

However, I have now come to believe that a mere list of causes and symptoms, no matter how coherent and comprehensive it may be, is not enough. What is missing from such an inventory—and indeed from all previous work in this field—is the dynamics of failure, the sequencing of events. We need a story-line that binds together all these causes and symptoms into a working model. This is what I hope to devise in the next chapter and so this chapter is merely a prelude to the next.

In this chapter, then, I shall present my list of lists which, as will be seen below, contains 12 main items. But even at this stage I think it is possible to see that these items have formed into a pattern, an embryonic story-line is already emerging and the items in the list are not just in a random order. Put as briefly as possible the 12 elements (in italics) are linked together in a mechanism that operates as follows:

> If the *management* of a company is poor then two things will be neglected: the system of *accountancy information* will be deficient and the company will not respond to *change*. (Some companies, even well-managed ones, may be damaged because powerful *constraints* prevent the managers making the responses they wish to make.) Poor managers will also make at least one of three other mistakes: they will *overtrade*; or they will launch a *big project* that goes wrong; or they will allow the company's *gearing* to rise so that even *normal business hazards* become constant threats. These are the chief causes, neither fraud nor bad luck deserve more than a passing mention. The following symptoms will appear: certain *financial ratios* will deteriorate but, as soon as they do, the managers will start *creative accounting* which reduces the predictive value of these ratios and so lends greater importance to *non-financial symptoms*. Finally the company enters a characteristic period in its *last few months*.

In the remainder of this chapter I shall describe each of these 12 items in more detail, but I must make one important point here that applies to all of them. This relates to the problem of visibility or verifiability. The main purpose of this book is to examine ways of predicting failure in the hope that we will be able to put forward some useful preventative or curative ideas in the final chapter. But all this effort is wasted unless the causes and symptoms I am about to list can be seen by managers and other observers. An invisible symptom is not much use. It is not much use talking about 'bad management' unless an observer can, on inspecting the company, see certain concrete facts indicative of bad management. It is not much use saying that 'poor management information' can be a cause of failure; we have to know exactly what figures in the company's books, or missing from the books, we should be looking out for. The list of 12 causes and symptoms below has to be judged by this harsh pragmatic criterion.

Management

There is wide or even universal agreement that the prime cause of failure is bad management. If the management is good, said several experts, only sheer bad luck can cause the collapse of the company. While I do not fully agree with this—see the summary above—I do agree that good managers will seldom make the same fatal mistakes as poor managers or, if they do make them, their managerial ability will protect the company from the worst consequences.

What precisely is meant by 'bad management'? We have now seen no less than six top management structural defects indicated by the experts: one-man rule, non-participating board, unbalanced top team, lack of management depth, weak finance function and combined chairman–chief executive. I believe one should be profoundly alarmed for the viability of any company exhibiting all these defects at once, for experience suggests that it would be in grave danger of making just those decisions that often lead to failure. Mitchell Construction apparently had all six faults. Rolls-Royce had five (it did not lack management depth). Penn Central had three. Let us summarize the six here.

ONE-MAN RULE

We must distinguish first between one-man rule and a one-man band. A one-man band is necessarily acceptable for a small company; the fact that it is small means that it may have only two directors, the proprietor and his wife, for example, where the chief executive unavoidably has to take all the decisions himself. That is a one-man band. 'One-man rule' is intended to describe chief executives who dominate their colleagues rather than lead them, who make decisions in spite of their hostility or reticence, who allow no discussion, will hear no advice. These men are autocrats—Henry Ford was mentioned, as were Ling, Cornfeld, Zanuck and many others. Not all autocrats are over-ambitious super-salesmen so set upon hyper-successful performance that they cease to believe in the existence of failure. Some are relatively retiring people who impose their will by their superior knowledge, as Sir Denning seems to have done in Rolls-Royce.

But, it will be said, what about all those autocrats whose businesses have not failed? What about the corporate heroes such as Walt Disney and Harold Geneen? And how does one know at what stage in the expansion of a one-man band the danger of one-man rule becomes severe? To these questions I have three answers, none of them very satisfactory. First, if there was a definitive answer it would by now be well known—Heaven knows, enough people have studied the subject of management over the past few decades—and we must learn the lesson now that there is no single reliable indicator for predicting failure. Second, although it comes down to a matter of personal judgement, I do think it is possible to tell the difference between a leader and an autocrat and between over-ambition and a normal desire to achieve. I also believe that one can divine the moment when a company has become too large to be safely ruled by one man—these questions are considered further in the final chapter. Third, the only way in which one man can dominate a company beyond the bounds of normal leadership is to ensure that as many as possible of the remaining five defects of management structure listed here are maintained. So these now become useful indicators that an autocrat sits on the throne.

NON-PARTICIPATING BOARD

Neither the board of Rolls-Royce nor that of Penn Central had the remotest idea how their company was performing. In neither case did the numerous bank chairmen who sat as outside directors recognize the symptoms of collapse until a few weeks before insolvency. Many of the experts were scathing about outside directors. But it is not only they who do not participate; many of the functional directors who sit on main boards, and many chief executives of subsidiary companies who do, take little part in discussions on matters affecting the company as a whole and only come alive when something is discussed that bears upon their particular special area of interest. (This phenomenon has to be experienced to be believed! Yet it is a universal feature of executive committees everywhere. Take Richard Crossman's remarks about how the British Cabinet works, 'We come [to Cabinet meetings] briefed by our Departments to fight for our departmental budgets, not as Cabinet Ministers with a Cabinet view.') Because of this phenomenon it is often all too easy for an autocrat to suppress discussion on any awkward reports that are not suppressed before they reach the board.

UNBALANCED TOP TEAM

The term 'top team' includes directors and very senior executives and advisers below director level. The phenomenon of imbalance is plainly visible in many engineering companies where not only is the chief executive an engineer but so are most of the board—several examples have been given here. This arrangement suits the autocrat, for none of his subordinates will challenge him on engineering decisions and all his subordinates are engineers. He is thus not challenged at all! As we shall see under 'Change' below, companies are threatened today by all manner of dangers from the technological to economic through the social and political. If the board does not contain a wide spectrum of skills then the chances of some new threat appearing but going unnoticed is severely increased.

WEAK FINANCE FUNCTION

A special case of unbalance in the top team, and in particular at board level, is a weak finance function. This may appear as a general phenomenon throughout the company resulting in inadequate financial and accounting controls as described below under 'Accountancy information'. But we have also seen, in the case of Rolls-Royce in particular, that even when these systems are perfectly adequate their message may not be heard at board level because the finance function is not strongly represented there. Many companies still have no finance director and only allow the chief accountant into a board meeting when the budget is being discussed.

LACK OF MANAGEMENT DEPTH

As with all these defects, this one also helps the autocrat to continue playing an exaggerated rôle in the company, but I confess to being less convinced that this defect is a useful indicator of possible failure. Rolls-Royce and Penn Central seem to me to have failed in spite of having a fairly adequate depth of management below board level, down to the shop floor. Furthermore, while I am fairly sure that I could, by careful inspection and inquiry, decide whether any of these other management defects were present in any given company, I am not sure I should know how to recognize a 'lack of management depth'—unless it was so glaring that the company would surely already be displaying other more obvious signs of distress.

CHAIRMAN–CHIEF EXECUTIVE

This defect is not only clearly visible, it is also, in my opinion, the most important one although only very few of our experts have mentioned it (Leach, Dunscombe, Heller and the Rolls-Royce inspectors). The point is this: if you draw the organization chart of a company's management you will see plainly that each manager is responsible to the manager above him. But to whom is the chief executive responsible? He used to be responsible to shareholders but as their power has waned it has left a vacuum at the top of the pyramid that today is filled by anyone who is able to fill it. Sometimes it is the government, sometimes the workers, but usually it is top management and often the chief executive himself. Sometimes he uses this double power prudently, sometimes he abuses it, sometimes he simply goes stale or makes a mistake. There is no one above him to shake him awake or divert him or warn him or dismiss him.

To sum up this section on the defects in management structure that appear to be frequently associated with failure, there appear to be six. One of these, management depth, I believe to be a poor indicator and substantially less important than the others. Of these, one is the main determinant of the other four; an autocratic chief executive will do his best to ensure that the defects in the management structure that allow him to remain an autocrat are perpetuated. Or, if a company has no autocrat but allows these defects to arise then an autocrat will surely emerge. If he does, the chances of that company now taking decisions that lead to failure are greatly increased.

Accountancy information

None of the contributors to our lists have suggested that managers lack physical information, such as output statistics or stock levels or sales by area or customer complaints. What is lacking in companies that fail is *accountancy* information. Four defects are particularly mentioned.

First, *budgetary control.* Well-managed companies draw up an annual (or even five-year) budget showing sales, revenues, interest payments, wages, rents, overheads, materials—and so on—in great detail, usually shown monthly or in 13 four-week periods. As the year goes by the accounts department publishes 'actual' figures which managers can compare with 'budget'. In this way variances can be identified and corrective action taken continuously. In poorly managed companies this system is not used or is defective or is entirely absent and the managers may not have the slightest idea whether the company is doing well or badly (see p. 19 concerning Cyril Lord). Budgetary control is of particular relevance for holding companies who do not wish to lose control of subsidiaries to whom they have delegated wide autonomy (see what Smith says on p. 20).

Second, *cash flow forecasts*. These are similar to budgets but show cash flows, bank balances, loans due to mature, profits, tax payments, etc. Again, in some companies these are absent, in other they exist but are not updated and a cash crisis can arrive unheralded.

Third, *costing systems*. Many companies do not know what each product costs to produce nor what effect it would have on profits if sales were increased by 10 per cent, say, nor what profit each subsidiary company is making. Unfortunately there are several different costs for each activity—marginal, opportunity and variable, for example—and very few managers really understand what all these are. Nevertheless, it appears that in companies that fail no costing figures of any sort are produced, or that they are manifestly inadequate or misleading or inaccurate.

Fourth, *valuation of assets*. This is an extremely difficult thing to do, partly because accountancy rules are necessarily loose and open to different interpretations, partly because inflation makes 'value' so flexible. It appears that incorrect valuation of assets is associated with failure (Rolls-Royce treated R&D as an asset, Penn Central overvalued its property, Mitchell Construction, Stirling Homex, and so on, all had these problems). I confess to being sceptical over this alleged defect. While I am sure that the correct valuation of assets is very difficult, I am not too sure that an incorrect valuation will often lead to failure. On the other hand, I am sure that a failing company will exaggerate asset values—but this is then a symptom of failure, not a cause. It should not come in this section, then, where we are concerned with causes (such as not having a budget or a costing system) but come under 'Creative accounting', below, which is a symptom.

I have faithfully listed four defects in information systems as suggested by the contributors, although I personally would exclude the last one.

What is important is that companies that fail may do so partly because they do not know where they are and do not know that they are failing. Or so the experts say. While I have no evidence that this is not true I have the impression that top managers always know whether they are failing or not, quite regardless of the efficiency of these formal information systems. However, the lack of adequate information systems will preclude other people seeing the approaching disaster and thus allow the top managers to hide their knowledge. The absence of reliable information also makes it difficult for anyone inside or outside the company to analyse its problems and evaluate alternative solutions. I would therefore certainly accept that this defect, in all its forms, but especially the first three listed above, is indicative of poor management and therefore of value in predicting failure. Even a relatively superficial inspection and inquiry is often enough to determine whether adequate accounting information systems exist in any given company.

Change

My thesis is that the more serious the defects in the top management structure of a company the higher will be the chances that two vital omissions will be made in the running of the company: the information system will be deficient as described above and, vastly more important, the company will not adequately respond to change.

I must make it clear that the changes I am discussing here are not the multitudinous ephemera of every day but the (relatively few) trends and events that strike at the core of a company's business, such as those mentioned by Ross and Kami, Simmonds, Smith, Houston, Cohen, Cork, Thorn and Scarlett. A company does not operate in isolation; it acts upon and reacts to a very complex environment which is continually changing, constantly moving. Some of these changes, such as population trends in peacetime, take place slowly and predictably. Others occur with such shocking suddenness and severity that no one can foretell how such a momentous event will change the shape of the world—as indeed was the case in 1973 when the Arab producers quadrupled the price of oil. Not to foresee such events or not to calculate their consequences, not to take note of such trends and their implications for one's business is a sure and certain way to failure.

It may be useful to place these changes into five main groups: those relating to the competitive, political, social, economic and technological environments. Under the heading of *competitive trends* or events, the emergence of foreign low-cost producers, the merger of two competitors, the announcement of a competitor's new range of products, the appearance of an entirely new company in your industry—all such changes are bound to have a profound impact, sooner or later, upon your company. Not to keep one's ear close to the ground or not to try to calculate and quantify the consequences and not to take appropriate action is certain to lead to a loss of competitive edge over a period of years.

Political change is relevant, too. Whether at the local level, where politicians may affect one's production resources, or at national or international level, where they can affect one's raw materials, markets and finance, politicians are playing a growing rôle in business all over the world. New quotas and duties and taxes and levies and legislation of all sorts pour out of government agencies like confetti. But more insidious, because they are not written down and published, are the changes in political attitudes towards business in general and certain industries and companies in particular. There is some reason to believe, for example, that Mitchell Construction failed partly because they did not recognize a change in government policy towards power station construction (p. 18).

Turning to *economic change*, managers have to consider such events as a devaluation of a major currency, an international monetary crisis, and so on, and such trends as the economic cycle, inflation, interest rates, patterns of disposable income and so on. At the time of writing, inflation is by far the most severe economic phenomenon. But while the poorly managed company has still not adopted inflation accounting, the well-managed company has not only done this but is already conducting a careful scrutiny of the economic scene to determine what their next major economic hazard might be. Also at this time the economies of Western nations seem to have become subject to a 4- or 4½-year economic cycle; it is probable therefore that any firm that is not habitually looking ahead at least five years will not be attuned to the fundamental rhythm of the economy in which it operates.

A similar, or even longer, time span is required to accommodate many of the *changes in society*. The attitude to work, for example, was seen to be changing a decade or more ago but many companies have still not really understood how profound is the movement towards 'participation' and 'job satisfaction'. Not to understand this and respond to it is to risk losing touch with one's employees, as perhaps Cornes Tideswell did (p. 25). A great number of companies have lost touch with their market or their customers because they did not see, or did not react to, such social trends as changes in life-styles, in composition by age or colour of a given population, in attitudes to pollution and consumer protection, and so on endlessly.

It is often said that *changes in technology* are the most influential today. While this must be true in some industries I personally believe it to be a very weak generalization. Nevertheless, Rolls-Royce did not respond soon enough to a change in technology and I have no doubt at all that many companies have failed for the same reason. (I think it is worth making the point that a company does not necessarily have to follow changes in technology; it is sometimes a perfectly valid response to decide not to follow a change but to move into an area of lower technology, or a different one—or, indeed, to adopt any of dozens of possible responses to a given technological change. It is also worth reminding ourselves of Cork's and Scarlett's opinion that no well-managed firm should be caught out by a change in technology even in these days of rapid change.)

Change, or rather failure to respond to change, is a major cause of collapse, then. The company either does not notice the change or does not respond correctly. Of course, some changes occur so suddenly and unpredictably that the company is wrong-footed and through no fault of its own, collapses. But this amounts to 'bad luck' and is, according to the experts and writers, only a very rare cause of failure, accounting for only one per cent or so. Nor do I believe that the rate of change has recently accelerated so far as to make life excessively difficult for the well-managed company as is the popular belief; that it has made life more difficult for the poorly managed company, I have no doubt. It is often possible to point to companies whose products or attitudes to employees or whose production facilities are manifestly so oldfashioned that the firm's failure is inevitable. No, I do not think that the accelerating rate of change threatens the well-managed company. What may threaten it is the growing number of constraints imposed upon business.

Constraints

In my opinion one of the most influential trends of the sixties was the emergence of an atmosphere almost of hostility towards companies on the part of the consumer, the employee, the state, students, and eventually even the man in the street. The demand that some form of accountability to society be devised for companies was heard all over the world. The belief that groups of people, other than shareholders, should draw a benefit from companies grew and spread, and the belief that groups of people should not be harmed by companies in the pursuit of profit gained wide acceptance. These new views became so strongly held and so widespread that the freedom of companies to respond to change was decimated. In America, for example, Ralph Nader, the consumer champion, obtained quite astonishing power—almost of veto—over the decisions of General Motors. One has only to consider the case of the Penn Central merger to see how a company can be strangled by the demands of many disparate groups of people all insisting upon achieving irreconcilable aims. I do not believe that Penn Central's failure was mainly due either to bad luck or to bad management; it was substantially due to the operation of constraints. (The management of Penn Central was certainly not good, but my belief, formed from studying the Senate report and Daughen and Binzen's book, is that it was not all that bad. Perhaps it is significant that Penn Central's top management displayed only three of the six defects listed under 'Management' above.)

Now I believe that, until recently, most companies confronted by a major change were well able to find a strategic response that would have been acceptable to all these groups and that failure from this cause was rare. But not today. There are three powerful new ingredients: the news media are happy to feature anyone who has a grudge against a company—especially if it is a well-known one; the trade unions, consumer organizations and other pressure groups have found a new cohesion and authority; national governments have joined the battle against companies instead of, as in the past, on their side.

Not to be able to merge for six years while the government argues with itself (Penn Central), not to be able to merge at all because the worker-directors veto it (Akzo-Phillips proposed merger in 1974), to have to subsidize the nation's exports out of one's profits (Rolls-Royce), not to be able to build an oil pipeline across Alaska for years while environmentalists argue, not to be able to develop an oil-rig construction site in Scotland, not to be able to close down a factory in Sweden, not to be able to raise prices (UK 1974), to be subjected to a ban on building property by the unions (Mainline)—all these are massive disabilities. Not to know whether the government wishes your company to make larger profits, or smaller, or none at all, is not conducive to dynamic business management. In short, I believe we have here a new, potent cause of collapse. It is so new that none of the writers and only one expert (Dunscombe) drew particular attention to it. It is so potent that, I believe, not even the best-managed companies can avoid being brought low by it if, by chance, their company moves into the sights of any one of these new powerful groups of people.

Whether one holds the view that these constraints have now become excessive or that, on the contrary, capitalism must be further controlled, is quite irrelevant. We have to deal with the world as it is.

To return to the main thesis, where we are concerned with the company in which the management structure is deficient, we have seen how two errors of omission will be made; it will neglect its accounting information systems and it will not adequately respond to change. The poorly managed company will also probably commit three other gross errors; it will overtrade, or it will launch a big project, or it will allow its gearing to rise.

Overtrading

A considerable number of writers and experts pointed to overtrading as a major cause of failure—see Leach, Paterson, Harvey, Curtis, Scarlett, Brough, Hartigan and Cohen. When a company expands it has to inject cash into stocks, debtors and other aspects of the business at approximately the rate at which the company as a whole is expanding. Thus if a company has a capital employed of £100 000 and is expanding at 20 per cent per annum then (as a crude over-simplification) it will have to find £20 000 in cash to finance stocks, debtors, advance payments, capital expenditure, and so on. Now, if that company makes a profit of £20 000—which is a fairly respectable 20 per cent return on capital employed—half will go in tax and half of the remaining £10 000 might go out in dividends, leaving enough cash to finance a mere quarter of its expansion. In other words, where a company expands faster than the internally generated cash flow expands, then the company has to borrow.

Collapse from overtrading can occur in several ways, of which two are interesting. The first strikes at healthy as well as unhealthy companies and arises solely because the managers underestimate the amount they must borrow or the time it may take to arrange the loans. Thus although the banks might be willing and able to grant a loan, there is simply not enough time to make the arrangements before, say, the wages have to be paid. I really cannot bring myself to believe that this happens very often or, if it does, that it brings about the failure of an otherwise viable enterprise.

The second definition of overtrading seems to me more convincing for it relates to the company which, in an attempt to expand, increases turnover at the expense of profit margins. Now, let us suppose that turnover increases faster than profits then, in any attempt to finance an increase in stocks, debtors, and so on with borrowed money, the income-gearing of the company (i.e., the amount of interest on the borrowings in relation to profits) will rise. No company can continue to do that for long without arousing the suspicions of their bankers who, on losing confidence in the company, will eventually decline to extend further credit. It is easy enough to fall into this overtrading trap unintentionally but a surprising number of managers, in their attempt to build a bigger empire, deliberately seek to increase turnover and share of the market—with scant regard for margins and profits. The setting of ambitious and challenging targets in terms of turnover and market share is a very common practice and one that is certainly to be encouraged. But in the wrong context or in the hands of managers who do not understand the need to set equally ambitious *profit* targets, it is the business equivalent of the Fools Mate in chess.

Although there was no hint of overtrading in the case of Rolls-Royce or Penn Central I think it is fair to claim that many of the companies Barmash described—Atlantic Acceptance, IOS, Equity Funding, for example—together with John Bloom, Cyril Lord, Stirling Homex, London and Counties, Piccadilly Estates, Wilstar Securities, Mainline Corporation, all failed, in part at least, from this cause. But I do not think they ran out of cash merely because they were expanding faster than the banks could advance the money. I do not accept this definition of overtrading. I think they ran out of cash because their banks realized that their increased turnover was coming from progressively 'lower-quality business', as bankers sometimes call it, and that their profits might not rise fast enough to cover the increased interest.

The big project

A considerable number of writers and experts mentioned the big project as a potent cause of collapse—Cork, Thorn, Curtis, Barmash, Brooks and Simmonds—and we know what happened to the RB 211, the Jetstream, the Penn Central merger, and the Kariba power station. There seems to be wide agreement, then, that one of the almost tediously repetitive mistakes that lead to failure is the big project where costs and times are underestimated or revenues overestimated. These errors always seem to be enormous—costs are never mildly greater, nor time schedules a little later, nor revenues slightly less than forecast—the miscalculations are monumental. I do not think this is due to mere chance and there are, I believe, a number of reasons why this should be so.

The first is tautological: if a company launches a big project where the cost and revenue forecasts are wrong only by a small margin then the project could probably be made profitable by an additional effort of management. If the errors are large then no amount of additional effort could bring the project round and the whole company might then fail. So of course the errors always seem enormous—companies that make only small mistakes do not go bust! But it is not as simple as that. I suggest that companies run by autocrats are much more likely than other companies to adopt grandiose schemes. If the accounting information systems are also faulty they are more likely to get their forecasts of costs and revenues wrong and more likely to remain ignorant of their mistakes until it is too late to correct them.

So I do not think we have a coincidence here or a tautology. I think we have, on the one hand, an association between healthy well-managed companies and a propensity to undertake projects that are within one's resources and, on the other hand, between poorly managed companies and a propensity to 'enter into obligations you may not be able to meet if things go wrong'—see Cork (p. 30).

My definition of a 'big project' includes a merger, a diversification programme, an expansion programme, the launch of a major new product or the introduction of a new service, a research programme, buying materials or components in bulk or as futures, and so on—i.e., not just physical projects such as building a factory—any undertaking or obligation that is large compared with the resources of the company.

It is an important conclusion of this book that while one may not normally be able to predict which project is going to fail—recall the Edsel and Project Intercept—one may be able to predict which company is going to fail.

Gearing

There are unfortunately a number of different definitions of this term, which is also called 'leverage' in the USA. It can mean the volume of long-term fixed-interest loans as a percentage of total capital employed; thus a company whose equity is valued at £100m and has raised £30m debentures has a gearing of 23 per cent (or 30 per cent by some calculations). Assume this company also has short-term loans (overdraft, for example) of £20m then, by some definitions, its gearing is £50m in £150 or 33 per cent (or £50m in £100m or 50 per cent). There are so many variations on this definition—do you include bonds, promissory notes, subordinated loan stocks, hire purchase, leasing, Eurodollars?—that I suggest we forget them all and think only about the wider implications. The fundamentals are that loans carry a fixed interest rate which does not depend upon how well or badly the company is doing while equity dividends do depend upon this. Also loans are (nearly always) ranked before equity in a winding up. Both these features mean that loans are normally a much cheaper source of capital than equity because the lender's interest and capital are both at less risk than the shareholder's dividend and equity. So the sensible, well-managed company funds as much of its business as possible with loan rather than equity.

There is a prudent limit, different for each business, beyond which the risks of high gearing outrun the advantages. The optimum point is determined by a number of factors including the legally binding terms of any deeds relating to debentures, the rate of interest expected on the various forms of loan, growth prospects and so on. Perhaps the most important determinant is the liability of the company's profits to extreme variations. Take Company A with no loans at all. It can be seen from Exhibit 7.1 that even in a bad year, when profits are half those in a good year, this company can still retain £15 000 to finance growth, provided it halves its dividend. But Company B which has an income gearing of 50 per cent in its good year (i.e., half its profits before tax go out in loan interest), is left with no dividend and no retained earnings at all in its bad year. This could lead to disaster because, to finance its operations in the following year Company B will have to borrow still more from the banks thus exacerbating its problem of high gearing. But Exhibit 7.1 was a gross oversimplification; let us, for example, assume that the reason that the profits of these two companies halved in the bad year was that there was an economic recession. If this was brought about by the government increasing interest rates, then as these companies' profits fall, interest rates rise, thus making the picture worse for both but *much* worse for B. See Exhibit 7.2. High gearing and an economic turndown are the classic nutcrackers of failure.

Exhibit 7.1. Table showing the effect of high gearing on retained earnings in a year in which profits are halved

	Good year		Bad year	
	Company A	Company B	Company A	Company B
Trading profit	100	200	50	100
Interest	—	100	—	100
Profit after interest	100	100	50	0
Tax at 50%	50	50	25	0
Profit after tax	50	50	25	0
Dividend	20	20	10	0
Retained earnings	30	30	15	0

Exhibit 7.2. Table showing the effect of high gearing coupled with high interest rates when profits are halved

	Good year		Bad year	
	Company A	Company B	Company A	Company B
Trading profit	100	200	50	100
Interest	—	100	—	140
Profit after interest	100	100	50	−40
Tax at 50%	50	50	25	0
Profit after tax	50	50	25	−40
Dividends	20	20	10	0
Retained earnings	30	30	15	−40

High gearing is a warning signal that no one should ignore; remember Rolls-Royce throughout the sixties; remember Penn Central as the merger approached and was consummated; remember what was said by Leach, Thorn, Curtis and Dunscombe. Let us also remember that providing your bankers have not lost confidence in you, they are only too pleased to let you gear your company to the rooftops.

It is part of my thesis, then, that poorly managed companies tend to gear up their equity beyond the prudent level so that their company is vulnerable not just to massive errors or strokes of gross misfortune but even to the normal hazards of business.

Normal business hazards

It is never sensible to push any analogy too far, but the collapse of a company is in some ways similar to the sinking of a ship. If a ship is in good condition and the captain is competent it is almost impossible for it to be sunk by a wave or a succession of waves. Even if there is a storm, the competent captain will have heard the weather forecast and taken whatever measures are needed. Only a freak storm for which quite inadequate notice has been given will sink the ship.

In view of this I suggest that a manager who blames an economic recession for his company's collapse is like a captain who has not heard the weather forecast. And what *does* that manager expect—a world without economic cycles? Some managers blame the government; perhaps an increase in a tax or some new legislation has 'caused' the failure. But again, what *does* he expect—a world in which taxes and laws are not changed? This is like the captain of a ship which is grossly overloaded blaming a two-foot wave for the sinking—and, in one sense, he is right; it *was* a two-foot wave that sank it! But what about all the other ships near by which are still afloat?

There are, then, certain events which by common consent do cause the failure of companies but which, being normal hazards of any business, ought not to cause it and indeed only do so because the company is already too weak to survive the blow. A strike at a supplier's premises, for example, ought not to cause a company's failure—suppliers often have strikes. A customer moves to a competitor—customers often move. There is a fire in a warehouse where your products are stored, a television personality mistakenly condemns your product, a director of your board is killed in an air crash. . . .

There must be a spectrum of events in which, at one end, the events are normal hazards while at the other end, there would be universal consent that the events or combination of events were sheer bad luck, a freak storm, against which no firm could have protected itself. While fully recognizing that bad luck can cause failure we should, I believe, also recognize that it is a very rare cause indeed; as for the normal business hazards, they can never be valid as an excuse for failure.

Financial ratios

I do not think there is any doubt that financial ratios are useful indicators of trouble and possibly of failure. A great deal of work has been done over the past several decades to establish the reliability of a number of financial ratios as indicators and the length of the list that follows is testimony to this work. And yet I have to declare three very severe doubts as to their usefulness in the study of corporate collapse. First, while these ratios may show that there is something wrong and while a sequence of them over time may show that it is getting worse, I doubt whether one would dare to predict collapse or failure on the evidence of these ratios alone. As a symptom of something wrong, yes; as a symptom of impending failure, no. Second, their value has been severely eroded by inflation. Figures that appear to show an improvement may conceal a deterioration in real terms. A ratio is essentially the comparison of one figure with another, and unless both figures are subject to the same rate of inflation, any comparison over time is invalid (see points 10 and 12 below). Third, as soon as the managers know that all is not well with their company, they will start creative accounting, thus hiding the tell-tale symptoms from everyone (perhaps even from themselves).

While these financial ratios are undoubtedly useful, then, they are not as useful as many people evidently believe and less reliance may be placed upon their predictive value than many people place upon them today. On the other hand, there are plenty of them:

1. Altman's Z which I have described in detail and which, I believe, would be extremely useful if managers calculated it for their company in normal times to establish a norm and then monitored its movements every few months.

2 to 6. The five ratios contained in Z but which might be well worth watching separately: working capital/total assets; retained earnings/ total assets; earnings before interest and tax/total assets; sales/total assets, and market value of equity/book value of total debt (a gearing ratio).

7. The 'current ratio' or current assets/current liabilities, which may show how readily the company could meet its short-term debts. Many companies like to see a ratio of 2:1 or better.
8. The 'quick ratio' or cash plus debtors/current liabilities, which even more stringently tests the company's ability to meet its short-term debts because, unlike 7, it leaves out stocks which might take some time to liquidate. It is often known as the 'acid test ratio' and many

firms like it at 1:1 or better (sometimes expressed as a percentage).

9. Profit/sales or 'margin'. This shows whether a company's profits are protected against a rise in costs or a fall in selling prices which often cause a 'profit squeeze' in times of economic downturn.
10. Sales/fixed assets. This ratio may indicate the extent to which the company is using its assets to generate turnover. But note that sales will be in the current year's £s while fixed assets may be in the £s of many years ago. Inflation will severely distort this figure if one is not careful to compensate for this error.
11. Cash flow/debt was found to be a useful predictor of failure by Beaver (see p. 60).
12. Stock + debtors − creditors/long-term capital is, according to Westwick in *How to Use Management Ratios*, a useful test of liquidity in times of inflation. If this ratio rises it indicates that the company will either have to raise new finance or it must increase its dividend cover by retaining a higher proportion of profits.
13. Long-term loans + equity capital/fixed assets is another of Westwick's suggestions (see Bibliography). This one shows whether the company's fixed assets, upon which its long-term future depends, are financed by equally long-term capital. A 1:1 ratio is prudent.
14. Price/earnings. The stock market capitalization divided by total after tax earnings gives the P/E ratio and reveals something of the stock market's opinion of the company's future prospects.
15. Share price/share index. Movements of a company's share price relative to the movement of the stock market as a whole (as measured by one of the well-known indices) may also indicate how the market currently views the company's prospects.
16. Various specialized ratios appropriate to each industry can be calculated such as the liquidity ratios in banking, ratios relating to capital and premium income in insurance, occupancy ratios in hotels, NOI/gross revenues in American railroads, etc.

My opinion is that if for each firm one selects a battery of appropriate ratios, including Z, and calculates what these have been in the past few years so that a norm can be established, there is a very good chance that they will give an early warning of trouble ahead. How much warning they might give is open to debate; some experts believe it is as much as five years. Others suggest two to three. Even two to three is much longer than most managers I have spoken to currently believe is possible. Yet several experts firmly believe this is frequently possible—Altman and Paterson among them. Apparently, then, financial ratios are useful alarm bells.

But I am also fairly sure that, however hard these alarm bells are ringing, everyone inside and outside the company will underestimate the urgency and seriousness of their message. The final failure will come as a complete surprise to everyone!

Creative accounting

A number of writers, including perhaps Ross and Kami (see Commandment 9, p. 13), appear to believe that creative accounting can cause the failure of a company. While I imagine it might occasionally happen that a company so confuses itself by juggling with its figures that it fails, I believe that creative accounting is generally a symptom of failure, not a cause.

The mechanism that brings it into play is quite simple. The top managers know, probably before they admit it to themselves and long before anyone else knows, that their company is not doing so well. They also know that if this becomes generally recognized the bank will tighten its credit terms, customers will begin to sidle away, suppliers will begin to demand cash on or before delivery. But worse than this the managers themselves will be seen to have failed. Their wives and children will see it. Then their friends. A hard knot of anxiety ties itself in their minds. They convince themselves that the stocks in the factory are worth so much more than last year, that the value of the buildings has risen remarkably, that bad debts will be much less, and that next year things will be very much better.

Next year things are not better. Yet they cannot further revalue the stocks or exaggerate the value of the buildings and they have now to resort to some of the more intricate devices I describe below. Later on things become worse still and the managers may then have to step over that ill-defined boundary between optimism and fraud. Whether they do so depends partly, I believe, upon the inner psychological make-up of the boss; if he is one of those who has an almost pathological need to succeed, not just once but again and again, then the steps across successive bands of untruth are probably taken quickly and without qualm. But whatever their psychology we must not forget that all businessmen are optimists and really do believe that 'the clouds will roll away' and that the firm must be kept alive until 'better times come' (see p. 46).

I have described a considerable number of creative accounting techniques ranging from the ingenious to the patently fraudulent and I reproduce some of them below collected together as a list.

1. Delay publishing the results for as long as possible. There are limits to this, legal ones in most nations, but it is rare not to be able to get away with a delay of at least one and perhaps two years. This is often enough; beyond that and either the company has failed or it has recovered. Delayed accounts, then, are a useful symptom for outside observers to watch for.
2. Capitalize research costs, either on the basis that these will be written off against orders already received or against orders expected to be received.
3. Continue paying dividends even if you have to raise equity or loans to do so. (While this may put shareholders off the scent it may not confuse investment analysts.)
4. Cut expenditure on routine maintenance until the plant is in such a poor state of repair that a major renovation is needed. This can be treated as capital.
5. In many nations leasing and hire purchase arrangements do not have to be shown as loans in company accounts. Although they are usually a very expensive source of capital their use does reduce apparent gearing.
6. Instruct all accounts departments to treat extraordinary income as ordinary and ordinary expenditure as extraordinary as far as possible. This of course improves current profits.
7. Instruct all subsidiaries to increase their dividends to the parent company. (If you have no subsidiaries you had better get some if you want to use this and number 8.)
8. Year by year bring into your consolidated accounts progressively more and more results, first from your 100 per cent owned subsidiaries, then 75 per cent, then 50 per cent.
9. Proprietors of small businesses should retain the company's main asset in their name or that of their wife. If the company fails most of the debts will then have to be met by the creditors. Outside observers —especially creditors!—should check this point for any suspect company.

10. Value your assets at whatever figure suits you. Either the auditors will not notice or, if you elect one of their partners to the board, they will say nothing.
11. It is not only research costs that can be capitalized; so can training costs, interest charges on loans, costs of setting up a computer, advance payments.
12. Inflation has seriously upset many accounting conventions. It should be possible to use it as a smokescreen in revaluing assets, for example.
13. Certain of a company's debts can be met out of the proprietor's own pocket. (This is especially useful to improve apparent profits just before a proprietor sells his shares!)
14. Value stocks of finished products at the current market selling price rather than at cost.
15. To impress one's bankers one could hold back a week's output so that, when they visit the factory, it appears to be a hive of activity.
16. Set up a Department 99 to invent some customers or some rice or ammonia or vegetable oil. If you need a ship to transport these goods, or tanks to store them in, invent these too.
17. Set a sales target for a given area of your business for a year. If sales fall short of this target, by say, 20 per cent, take 20 per cent of that area's expenditure out of the current year's accounts and defer it to next year.
18. Do not revalue your assets so that, although your provision for depreciation looks adequate compared to their book value, in fact it is much too low.

Now all these devices are intended to make a company's results look *better* than they really are. I must point out that most companies do not *want* their results to look better. The more profit they publicly declare the more tax they pay and the greater will be union pressure for wage claims. So whenever one finds a company deliberately taking measures to improve their results one may assume either that they are very concerned about their share price or about to go out for a loan or any of several entirely satisfactory reasons—plus one most unsatisfactory one, namely that they are going bust. Thus creative accounting becomes one of the most useful symptoms of impending failure. Thus we should take the advice of Mr Allen (p. 36) and take the annual accounts of any suspect company to pieces, not to see what the figures are, but to see if there is any evidence of creative accounting. To discover that the profits should be £1·8m rather than £2·7m as published is admittedly interesting; what is even more interesting is that someone has taken the trouble to mislead us. So creative accounting itself becomes a symptom as well as a smokescreen. 'Where there is smoke there is fire.'

I have come to believe that this phenomenon is almost invariably associated with failure—we even had creative accounting in the twenty-second largest company in England and the sixth largest in America. I suspect that it is one of the most reliable of all the symptoms. I am equally sure that nearly all non-failing firms do their best to present honest accounts (not forgetting the huge latitude that even the best accounting conventions allow, especially in times of inflation) and that nearly all proprietors and managers of failing companies who adopt creative accounting techniques do so from the best of motives. To keep the company afloat until the clouds roll away. Not for dishonest reasons, not for fraud, not for personal gain—at least no more so in companies that are failing than those that are not.

We must be clear, however, that creative accounting, once it begins, severely diminishes the predictive value of the financial ratios since these ratios are nearly all based upon figures that creative accounting seeks to distort. Lest there is any doubt as to how severe this effect can be consider this sequence of quick ratios (or acid tests, see p. 138) for a certain company.

	%
1969	96·9
1970	82·5
1971	56·9

This construction company failed in 1972. It is clear that in 1971 there was a severe reduction in liquidity. But these calculations are based on the published accounts. If you make the adjustments, however, you get the following quick ratios:

	%
1969	54·0
1970	30·7
1971	21·7

In this case, then, a casual observer would not have worried about this company's liquidity until 1971 (or rather, until the publication of the

1971 accounts in 1972) whereas perhaps he should have been worried right back in 1969 (because most companies like to see the quick ratio at around 100 per cent).

This is what I believe: most healthy companies publish neutral accounts, and ratio calculations based on them may therefore be relied upon. Almost all companies that are not healthy do attempt to conceal the truth in their published accounts and all ratios calculated from these are unreliable. This phenomenon is almost invariable and largely explains why it is that so many people, some of them highly skilled in financial and company affairs, do not appreciate how serious are the difficulties of suspect companies (i.e., companies they know to be in some difficulty) until almost the day on which insolvency is announced. It also explains why, when the collapse occurs it is more severe than anyone expected.

A further implication is that if creative accounting diminishes the value of financial ratios, one has then to rely more heavily upon non-financial symptoms.

Non-financial symptoms

If the writers and experts are correct, and a considerable volume of confirmatory evidence emerged from the various case studies, a large number of non-financial symptoms are displayed by failing companies. Unfortunately, and this the writers and experts did not say, a great number of them are also displayed by companies that are not failing although admittedly not many are seen in companies that are highly successful.

Take 'low morale', for example. This is certainly a symptom of a company that is recognized by its employees not to be successful or to be failing. However, low morale can exist in a relatively successful company and conversely even in a company quite close to failure morale might be high. These arguments apply to nearly all the non-financial symptoms discussed here but I believe that, in spite of this, they do have some confirmatory value in predicting failure.

Of particular interest may be the demeanour of the top managers. If it is true that they are normally the first to realize that the company is in trouble then one of the earliest symptoms may be their furrowed brows and bad temper. (According to Daughen and Binzen, during Saunders's last few weeks as chief executive of Penn Central his hands shook uncontrollably.) Allen and Scarlett both suggest that a visit to the company to meet the top managers is useful. Employees and visitors alike may be able to see such rather obvious symptoms as dingy offices, poor maintenance, and a general air of financial stringency.

Customers will note a decline in quality or service, price cuts and the firm's tightening credit policies. Suppliers will notice that the firm is running down stocks of components or materials or reducing the size of orders, or taking longer to pay. Employees will observe the greater resistance to pay increases, cuts in overtime and less generous treatment generally, delays in capital expenditure authorizations, rising stocks, the outdated product, the declining market share, the growing volume of customer complaints and an increasing desperation among the top, and later the middle, management.

All these people and groups of people—together with the bank manager anxiously watching the overdraft and the firm's accountants anxiously watching the financial ratios and the stock exchange gradually marking down the shares—all these people will see that something unusual is happening and will marvel and wonder at it but keep their peace. For while they each hold a part of the jigsaw, none of them, except the chief executive, can see the whole puzzle. Except perhaps the outside directors who, having had an excellent boardroom luncheon, are sound asleep.

I do not propose to construct a long list of these non-financial symptoms because they will be different for each industry and even each company. Suffice it to say that a trained or knowledgeable observer could almost certainly see a great number of them in any failing company if he took Allen's advice, 'Go there'. He could gather even more if he spoke to customers and suppliers, employees and managers. All the signs are there. The trouble is that so very few people are in a position to recognize them for what they are.

The last few months

In the last few months before insolvency the number and severity of the symptoms rapidly increase. The stock market will by now certainly have marked the shares down, perhaps to a fraction of their previous levels. Even at this late stage, however, the top managers are protesting loudly that all is well, that the embarrassment is temporary or non-existent. Remember Sir Denning, seven months before insolvency, saying 'The company is in good shape.' The more flamboyant chief executives appear in public surrounded by an even more lavish bevy of dolly girls than usual, just to prove conclusively that everything is fine, just fine. The banks rally round with further loans—remember Rolls-Royce and Penn Central? Normal dividends continue to be paid out.

Each new item of news about the company and its affairs both financial and operational becomes worse than the last but still the full magnitude of its problem is not understood because the most recent published accounts showed that things could not be that bad. But soon the suppliers are demanding cash on delivery, creditors are asking questions and shareholders are seeking reassurance. The bank's representative calls. Near the end, perhaps only a matter of days before it, the proprietor of the small firm is on his knees, metaphorically at least, to his bank manager, his friends, his wife, his customers, his suppliers, his pawnbroker; the chief executive of the big firm is at Number Ten and the international telephone cables are buzzing with negatives. By now it is too late to effect a rescue—it has been too late for months, probably—and either the creditors, or more often the banks, call in the Receiver who, usually, is greeted not with hostility by the top managers, but with relief. And, as we have learnt, the Receiver nearly always finds that, while the company as it was can never be profitable, there nearly always is a profitable core.

Although the events of the last few months are of only academic interest to us—for by this point it is normally far too late to take effective action other than calling in the Receiver—I felt my description of the process of collapse would be incomplete without it. And it is remarkable how often this melodrama is repeated, almost word for word so to speak, every time a company, large or small, moves towards insolvency. That this happens with such remarkable similarity each time is a reflection, I believe, of the widespread use of creative accounting in failing companies. This so effectively postpones the evil day that when it does come, it cannot but be dramatic. This is a point that a number of interested parties might do well to remember.

First, the shareholders who, by the time this last undignified scramble for cash is taking place will almost certainly have lost their capital. Second, the creditors, who by now will be bearing the full brunt of any further losses during this period—often quite a long period. Third, for anyone thinking of buying or merging with a failing company the old advice of *caveat emptor* is highly appropriate even before this last slide into insolvency has begun. Not to look most carefully behind the accounts, as opposed to merely looking at them, is to invite disappointment or worse. Fourth, for anyone thinking of bailing out a company that is about to call in the Receiver or has just done so—whether it is government or supplier or customer or worker cooperative—this same warning applies but with even greater force, for you may be sure that any figure that is suggested as being required to keep the company going is a gross understatement of the true requirement.

8. *Three trajectories*

In the previous chapter I presented my list of 12 causes and symptoms culled from the writers and experts and the case studies described in earlier chapters. I suggested that these items had already begun to form into a coherent story-line and had ceased to be merely 12 separate items in a list. The scenario of failure that they seemed to me to be spelling out went something like this.

Companies which display certain defects in *management* structure associated with one-man rule tend to make two errors of omission and three of commission. The two of omission are the neglect of *accountancy information* systems and, worse, the failure to respond adequately to long-term *changes* in their environment. The three of commission are a tendency to *overtrade* or to launch a *big project* that is beyond their resources or to allow their *gearing* to increase so that even *normal business hazards* are a constant threat. Some companies, even quite well managed ones, can now be severely damaged by *constraints* upon their choice of response to change. As a company slides down the path to insolvency its *financial ratios* deteriorate, it begins to employ *creative accounting*, certain *non-financial symptoms* appear and it finally enters a dramatic *last few months*.

I believe that this story-line is already of considerable practical value in identifying companies that are liable to failure or who have started on the long downward path itself—I say 'long' because one of the facts we have also learned is that the process of failure often takes at least a few years to complete. Imagine a senior manager applying this story-line to his own company. He knows the chief executive rules the board with a rod of iron and has done so for years, he knows the board never looks at the monthly budget variance reports, he knows that two years ago their brilliant chief designer died and their new range of products will be severely delayed, he knows that turnover has been rising very rapidly due to the company cutting selling prices. . . . He can see how four of our fatal items have already appeared and he will look, with acute anxiety no doubt, to see if any more are apparent. Imagine his horror when, a few months later, he receives a confidential memorandum from the accounts department asking him either to reduce maintenance costs in the factory or to record them as capital!

I suggest, then, that my list of 12 items not only includes all the most reliable items from other lists, and excludes unreliable and unimportant ones such as fraud and bad luck, but is also alive instead of dead. It is dynamic instead of static. Furthermore it embraces causal agents as well as symptoms and this is important because symptoms only occur *after* a company has started upon the downward slide while potential causes, such as the six management defects, are present *before* failure begins. But there is one very serious deficiency; not all companies display all these features nor do they all follow exactly the same route to insolvency. Indeed some follow a path that is markedly different from others. How many typical paths are there? There are three. Is it possible to say which company will follow which path? Yes, I think it is.

Three types of failure

The idea that there must be several very different paths, or trajectories as I shall call them, each capable of being described in considerable detail, occurred to me soon after visiting Mr Harvey. It was he who described several examples of companies which failed without ever making any profits; at the same time I was reading Altman's book and was surprised to read how many firms that failed were less than five years old—well over 50 per cent. Also at the same time, I happened to meet a senior

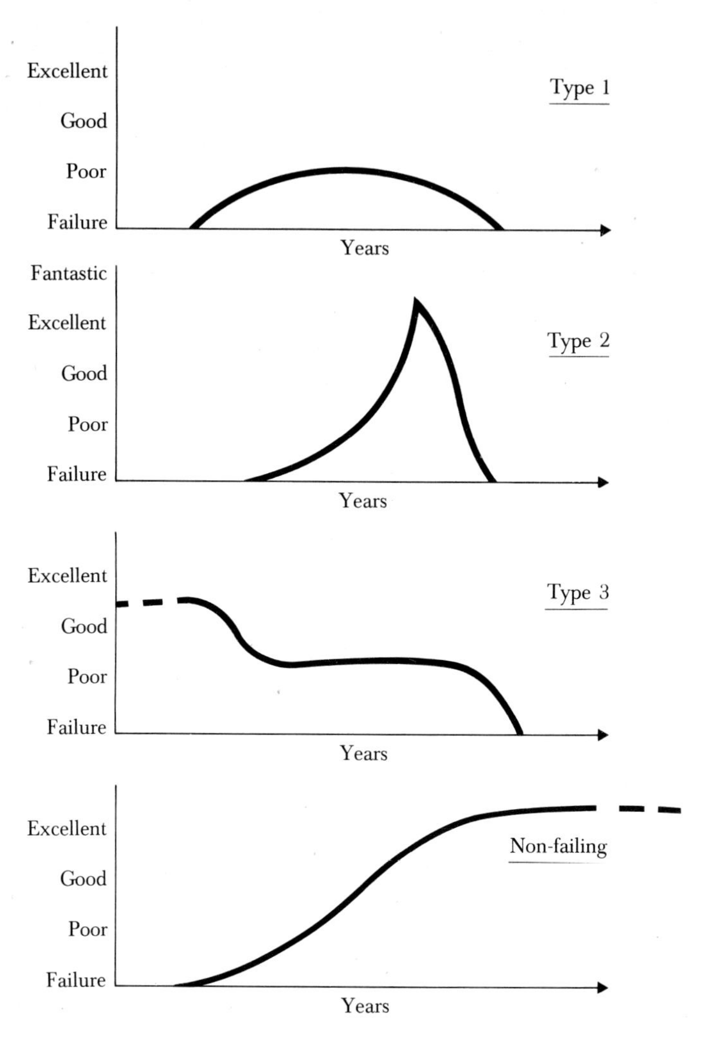

Exhibit 8.1. The three types of Failure Trajectory

employee of a company that was formed to launch a new sports car into the UK market, and the company, Strada Cars, failed some months later aged 3½ years.

Now here we have several cases of companies failing because they 'never got off the ground'. And yet Barmash describes a number of company failures which certainly form a cateogry of their own but which could hardly be more different from these. The Barmash companies certainly got off the ground! So that gives two different possible trajectories. Are there any more? I think Rolls-Royce is different again. Rolls-Royce certainly got off the ground—it was a highly profitable company for several decades—but it did not collapse like the Barmash companies. So there are certainly three types of failure; are there any more? There may be, but I believe that these three describe such an enormous percentage of all failures that to attempt to identify a fourth would lead more to confusion than enlightenment.

I shall describe the three in detail below but an approximate outline of each is shown in Exhibit 8.1. It will be seen that the Type 1 failure follows a very low profile, indicating that its performance never rises above 'poor' before sinking into the arms of the Receiver. Type 2, on the other hand, shoots upwards to 'fantastic' heights before crashing down again as did IOS, Atlantic Acceptance, Stirling Homex, and others. Type 3 is a rather more complex trajectory; these companies have usually been going for years or decades so the start and early years are not shown. We only become interested in these mature companies at the end of a period of 'good to excellent' performance where there is a partial collapse, followed by a plateau (in the case of Rolls-Royce this lasted for nearly a decade from the partial collapse in 1961) after which there is a rapid decline to insolvency. As a comparison I have also shown in Exhibit 8.1 the trajectory for a healthy non-failing company which follows the well known S-curve consisting of a slow start, a rapid build-up and then an indefinite period of stable 'good to excellent' performance.

If there really are three types of failure and if they really are as different from each other as I am suggesting, why has this not been noticed before? I can only suppose that each expert sees only one type of failure. Thus the journalists are mainly interested in the drama and ballyhoo that always surrounds the Type 2 company. Managers are mainly interested in the mature, professionally managed Type 3. No one is particularly interested in the Type 1 failures because they are small and insignificant—except to the small, local accountancy firms like Mr Paterson's. But these firms only act as Receivers to Type 1 failures and would seldom see a Type 2 or 3. And large accountancy firms will seldom handle a small Type 1. My explanation then, is that the expert's knowledge is so specialized that none of them see the full range of failure and no one before has brought all the experts' views together in one place.

What does seem certain is that any one who reads Barmash's book, and only that, will firmly believe that all failure is caused by greed and fraud. Anyone who talks to the big accountancy firms, and only to them, will believe that failures are largely caused by lack of accountancy skills. Managers will convince you that bad management is the cause. Managers whose companies have failed will tell you that it was the government's fault. But each of these statements is naïve because one can instantly think of examples of failure which decisively invalidate them. I doubt if any statement can be valid for all company failures—which range, let us remember, from the huge and ancient Penn Central to the backstreet builder—and that must mean that there are several different types of failure, or, to be more precise, that several different types of company fail in different ways.

No wonder those lists we saw in the early chapters were so different; all the authors were talking about different types of company! And that also explains why we saw so few of their listed items in the case of Stirling Homex (p. 23)—none of them had experience of a Type 2 failure. Most of the authors of those lists were professional managers or accountants whose experience was mainly limited to mature professionally managed Type 3 companies—so no wonder their listed items were so well confirmed by the Rolls-Royce and Penn Central cases.

The concept of 'trajectory'

I have already explained why a mere list seems to me an inadequate weapon in the prediction of failure because it does not describe the sequence in which causes and symptoms may be expected to occur. This is why I prefer to use a trajectory so that the story-line may be represented in a diagram. Each of the three types of failure follows a different sequence; each is marked by a different combination of causes and symptoms which, I believe, are unique to the type. If this is so, then a trajectory diagram for each type, each labelled with its own sequence of causes and symptoms would have very considerable predictive value. The management of a large mature company, knowing that if their company is going to fail it will do so by reproducing the Type 3 trajectory, and knowing that symptoms A, B and C associated with the early part of that trajectory have already been observed, will watch for D and, if it appears on cue, will be warned to take urgent action. (Prevention and cure will be considered in the next chapter.)

What is a trajectory? It is a line on a graph which is intended to represent the general health of a company. I must make it clear that this line does not represent any one indicator of corporate health such as profits or turnover. No doubt profit and turnover would follow the trajectory line quite faithfully since both are quite good indicators of health but I prefer not to rely on only one or two indicators. There are three reasons for this. The first is that profits or turnover are both subject to marked fluctuations from year to year, while I do not think corporate health does fluctuate over such a short period. The second is that, as we now know, failing companies usually employ creative accounting techniques to 'improve' profits and other key indicators. The third is that there are a number of indicators of health which are just as useful as profits, namely stock market share values, return on capital, employee morale, reputation with customers and suppliers and so on. We should make use of them.

It would be extremely useful if we could measure all these indicators accurately and then amalgamate them mathematically into a composite indicator of corporate health, but of course we do not know how to do this and the trajectory line is therefore a somewhat subjective construction from all these individual indicators.

So the trajectory is an indicator of the general health of a company as it collapses towards insolvency plotted against time. Where possible I have shown the time scale on the horizontal axis. On the vertical axis I have identified five states of health: *failure* (i.e., where the Receiver is called in), *poor*, *good*, *excellent* and *fantastic*. In the descriptions of each of the three types below I shall use the trajectory as a backbone on which to hang labels, each in its proper place, describing the causes and symptoms associated with that type. These will be numbered in sequence.

Detailed description of Type 1

Type 1 failures occur only to companies newly formed and, almost invariably therefore, affect only small ones. Altman, however, describes a company, which I would certainly classify as Type 1, which was launched with a capital outlay of $17m (p. 69). The Type 1 trajectory is low and brief. The general health of the company probably never rises above 'poor', and it probably fails within five years (some, such as the one Altman describes, last only two years while others, such as Lanchester (see p. 19) last as long as eight).

At Point 1 on the Type 1 trajectory (see Exhibit 8.2), i.e., at the launch of the company, a number of defects in the management structure will be seen. There will be one-man rule for the simple reason that, in most cases, the company may only have one manager at that early stage and consequently there will also be a lack of management depth, an unbalanced top team—and all the other six defects listed under 'Management' on p. 123. It may seem unfair and even ridiculous to list these as defects when, almost by definition, a newly formed company cannot have a vast array of highly trained executive directors. It may be unfair, but a defect it remains; companies fail, even small companies fail, because the top management

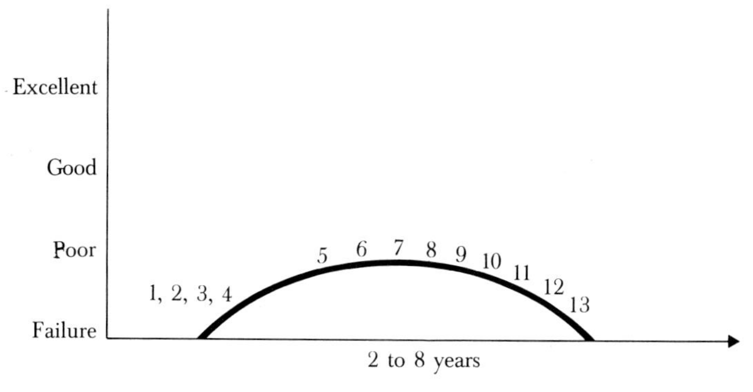

Exhibit 8.2. The Type 1 trajectory

team—in this case the proprietor alone—is not adequately equipped with the wide knowledge and skills that are now required to be successful in business.

The presence of an autocrat in a company is an important indicator of possible failure. But in the case of a one-man band we have to interpret with care for the boss of a small company is bound to dominate it without it necessarily coming to any harm.

Also at the very start of the company's history we will be able to see other defects, at Point 2, relating to accounting information (see p. 126). There will be no budget, no cash flow plans, no costing system. The proprietor will almost certainly not have included loan interest, depreciation, and so on, in the few calculations that he has made. He will not have allowed for losses in the early years. He will not know the marginal cost of his product. He may never have heard of 'contribution'.

At Point 3, also in the very early days, he will either obtain a bank loan (remember Altman's amazing example on p. 69 and Thorn's on p. 34?) or bought equipment on hire purchase. So the gearing will be high right from the start. Perhaps he will have retained some assets in his own name thus further increasing the effective gearing.

At Point 4, still in the earliest days, the company launches a big project. Now this may also be thought unfair for the 'big project' I refer to is the launch of the very product or service that the company was formed to launch. The project *is* the company—so of course it is big compared to its resources! But we must not forget the definition of the big project; this included the warning, made by many experts, that the costs and times are always grossly underestimated and the revenues grossly overestimated. It is these errors that often cause the project to become a massive burden on a company's resources, not always the original intended size of the project.

These Type 1 companies, then, begin life with four serious defects. Right from the start four out of the seven causal agents of failure, listed in chapter 7, are present at birth. I must stress that not every new company has these defects; many proprietors do not borrow excessively, many do not launch their new product on such a scale that its requirements exceed their resources, many do recognize that their knowledge of finance, say, or pricing policy, is inadequate and seek advice from an accountant or marketing expert. I believe, then, that only a relatively superficial examination is required to identify the potential failure candidates. These will have a proprietor whose knowledge is unbalanced, who has no accounting systems and who has geared up heavily. It may even be possible to see, right from the start, that the task the company has undertaken is too great although, more usually, one would have to wait for confirmation of this at Point 5.

At Point 5 it becomes clear that the proprietor has in fact seriously underestimated the cost and overestimated the revenues of the project the company was formed to launch. Point 5 may well occur within months of the start of the company—remember we are not discussing some minor miscalculation that a little extra overtime will put right. We are discussing a monumental mistake; not a few per cent but an order of magnitude or two. It should not be too long therefore before it is realized that the company must sell not 100 units a week to make a profit, as was originally calculated, but 150 units or 200 units. From now on the company will have to make a heroic effort just to exist; yet the proprietor cannot contemplate the ignominy of going into liquidation so soon after starting up. Furthermore, he will tell himself, the company is young, the product has only just been launched and sales are rising.

But the cash flows are probably still negative and so are profits at Point 6; all the financial ratios look poor, too. At Point 7 the proprietor may begin creative accounting because he expects to have to ask the bank for a further loan. At Point 8 even the most insensitive of wives will see signs of strain in their husbands and several other non-financial symptoms will appear. At Point 9 a normal business hazard occurs, such as a strike or an economic turndown. At Point 10 the proprietor takes some form of crisis action such as cutting the selling prices to customers thus increasing turnover, leading to overtrading. At Point 11 he seeks further loans although his net assets are probably already negative and goes through the usual, but very painful, last few months. Either he obtains more capital, in which case at Point 12 he finds he cannot make enough profit to maintain the interest payments, or he does not; in either case the Receiver is called in at Point 13.

It would be quite absurd to suggest that all Type 1 failures occur exactly and precisely in this manner. Not all of them, for example, will overtrade at Point 10; some will not overtrade at all. Not all of them will be making losses at Point 6; some will never make losses but will earn such exiguous profits that they cannot carry on. However, the main feature of Type 1 failures, that they 'never got off the ground', is well illustrated in the above description and many of the causes and symptoms noted will certainly occur, often in the sequence above, in typical Type 1 failures. Type 1 failures are by far the most common—over 50 per cent and perhaps as many as 60 per cent of all failures are of this type.

In some cases, then, one may be entitled to predict failure right from the start, for such companies are presented with the following dubious gifts on their birthday: an unbalanced top team (of one man) with a weak finance function and no management depth; rudimentary budgetary control, costing systems and cash flow plans; high gearing; and a project well beyond their means. Even if one cannot at this early date be sure that the proprietor's forecasts are wildly optimistic one may obtain confirmation of these suspicions within months of the launch of the company's product, i.e., by Point 5.

Only two of the 12 items listed in chapter 7 do not feature in Type 1 failures. One is *change*; most Type 1 companies do not survive long enough to be brought down by a failure to respond to long-term changes. The other is *constraints*. Most Type 1 companies are too small to be severely affected by pressure groups or governments. I do not exclude these two items from Type 1 failures but I suspect their influence to be small and occasional.

Detailed description of Type 2

Type 2 failures also occur to very young companies although they usually survive longer than Type 1. The briefest we have seen was Stirling Homex

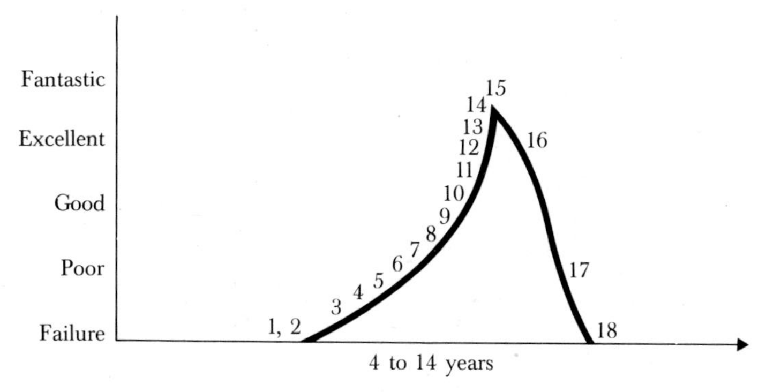

Exhibit 8.3. The Type 2 trajectory

(four years) while IOS collapsed after 14 years. I guess the average is less than 10 years. The trajectory is wholly different from Type 1; here the company most certainly 'gets off the ground'—indeed it almost loops the loop (see Exhibit 8.3).

At Point 1, where the company is formed, we can see the same management defects as in Type 1—all six of the management structural deficiencies are present for exactly the same reason as in Type 1, namely that these companies are started by one man and his wife or brother or friend and a few employees. But there is one very prominent and identifiable difference, namely that while the proprietor of a Type 1 company is not notable for his outstanding personality, the proprietor of a Type 2 is. So remarkable is this feature, which Barmash particularly noticed, that I shall record it as Point 2. While the Type 1 proprietors are engineers, technicians, marketing men, hairdressers, welders, builders and other mortals, Type 2 proprietors are super-salesmen; they are leaders of men, flamboyant, loquacious, restless and bubbling with ideas. The scale of their ambition is almost pathological. They never accept advice, they 'know it all'.

Very early in the company's history, at Point 3, it becomes clear that the energy and ability of the proprietor, together with what is often a brilliant product, has ensured a swift take-off. At this early point, then, Type 2 trajectories diverge from Type 1. Sales continue to expand rapidly (Point 4) necessitating new capital resources and, since margins do not fall and since the proprietor's powers of persuasion are considerable, these resources are readily made available (Point 5). No overgearing or overtrading occurs. On the contrary, by now a number of financiers and institutions are becoming interested in the remarkable performance of the company and offers of capital are received in some profusion (Point 6). Sales and profits continue to rise (Point 7).

(I must add that, at around this stage, the unscrupulous 'company pusher' occasionally appears. He offers his own capital to the entrepreneurs, trumpets the company's brilliant future, and then, just before the company collapses, sells out. Sometimes it is his selling out that contributes to the collapse just as it was his trumpeting that earlier contributed to the peak value of its shares. I am fairly sure that a company pusher was operating in one of the examples mentioned in an earlier chapter.)

Up to this point the Type 2 company's trajectory, while now very different from Type 1, is not so very different to an unusually promising example of the non-failing trajectory I suggested in Exhibit 8.1. But now, at what I shall call Point 8, a promising company's trajectory, having reached 'good' would begin to curve over and settle down to a long, sober, stable period between 'good' and 'excellent'. But Type 2 companies do not do this. Instead, the volume of sales, the level of profits, the availability of capital and other resources all continue to expand. At Point 9 the company is noticed by the press and a vicious circle is completed; now the company *has* to succeed because it is publicly expected to, so it has to sell more, so it has to borrow more, so it has to succeed more. By Point 10 the company is now so large and important that any normal company would long ago have introduced all the trappings of formal management. Type 2 companies continue being run by the proprietor who perpetuates all or most of the six management defects. At Point 11, whether it has 'gone public' or not the proprietor himself is now extremely wealthy and his name is known throughout the land. But this merely means that the super-star performance must continue unabated. Its general health is now so much better than 'excellent' it can only be called 'fantastic'.

At Point 12 turnover grows again—but this time profits do not. No one knows that this inevitable turning point has been reached because creative accounting begins immediately at Point 13. In a frantic attempt to keep turnover and profits rising at the rate that the proprietor, his backers, his public, his employees have come to expect he now reaches into the absurd. It was at Point 14 that John Bloom was launching his Bulgarian holidays, his trading stamps, his home movies and was making enough washing machines per week to sink the British Isles. Cyril Lord was launching his astrakhan, his plastic grass, his retail shops. Bernie Cornfeld's IOS controlled so many shares that within a matter of years he would rule the world. Billie Sol Estes had invented so much ammonia that the tanks required to hold it would have blotted out the American countryside—some one was bound to notice that the tanks weren't there! Atlantic Acceptance had lent money to everyone who could ever pay it back and had to start lending to those who could not. Beyond the clouds lie the stars. Beyond the stars lies the Great Absurd.

At Point 14, then, we find the most entertaining non-financial symptom, namely that the company and its proprietor have become ridiculous. Technically they are overtrading, for turnover has now risen so long and so fast that the bankers begin not to believe their luck and, at Point 16, they refuse further advances. But Point 16 is on the downswing of the trajectory; something happens at Point 15 to turn it down. What that is varies enormously from company to company. Sometimes it is a normal business hazard. For John Bloom it was that his new product was unreliable, his selling costs had risen while his competitors' had fallen. For Bernie Cornfeld it was a turndown in world stock markets.

The collapse is now quite swift, partly because once the press scent trouble there is no hiding it from the banks or the stock market. No amount of denial or creative accounting can stop the collapse to Point 17, the last few months, then to Point 18 where the Receiver is called in.

In the case of Type 2 failures only very few of the 13 items in my list play a major part. The management defects do. Overtrading does, creative accounting does and the last few months are typical. But the lack of accounting information does not seem to matter, nor do Type 2s neglect their response to change. Constraints seldom affect them, they do not overgear, they do not launch a big project that fails, financial ratios do not seem to be of any predictive value, perhaps because the collapse occurs so suddenly. I know of no reliable non-financial symptoms other than the company's headlong flight into the realms of absurdity.

In spite of the dearth of symptoms and in spite of the suddenness of the collapse of these companies, I believe that the trajectory described above does allow us to predict their probable failure long before the peak and turndown at Point 15. The critical period for prediction is where the Type 2 trajectory diverges from the non-failing trajectory at Point 8. While there is no physical event that anyone may observe to mark this point, I believe that any observer who has followed the progress of a company and compared it with my standard Type 2 trajectory through all the previous seven points, will be able to judge when Point 8 has been reached. Normal non-failing companies, however successful, do not grow at the rate these do at this stage.

One other matter must be emphasized: this type of failure is extremely rare. I doubt if there will be more than one or two in the UK in a normal year. But they attract attention far beyond their social or economic significance because of the squeals of delight from the press on their way up the trajectory—and again on the way down! They become nearer to show business than business. But I have included them here as a separate type because so many people who read the press or who read only books on failure by journalists will be labouring under the misapprehension that this is the way all companies fail. If this belief is held by a manager or a serious observer of a normal company then he will be watching and searching for quite the wrong symptoms.

Detailed description of Type 3

Type 3 failures occur only to mature companies which have been trading successfully for a number of years or decades. Sometimes they are still quite small, often they are sufficiently large to have a formal management hierarchy and occasionally they are enormous national institutions, of which Rolls-Royce and Penn Central are examples. Not only are these companies of some social and economic importance to the local or national or even international community but the number of Type 3 failures is

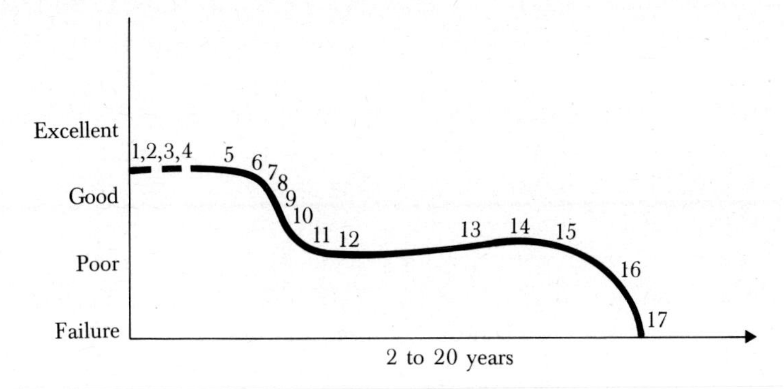

Exhibit 8.4. The Type 3 trajectory

considerable—probably between 20 per cent and 30 per cent of all failures are of this type. (Recall that 20 per cent of all failures are of companies more than 10 years old; most of these would be Type 3 and so would some less than 10 years old but more than 5 years.)

Because they have traded successfully for a number of years I shall not show their start-up trajectory at all. All we need do is to note at Point 1 on the Type 3 trajectory (see Exhibit 8.4) that the typical company's health has been and remains 'good to excellent' with turnover rising soberly in real terms, profit margins good, gearing low, morale good and so on. But at Point 2 we must record that several defects in the management structure exist, namely one-man rule or chairman–chief executive or unbalanced top team or non-participating board or lack of management depth or weak finance function. Our anxiety is proportional to the number of these present—recollect that these are mature companies, most of whom should by now have ceased to rely solely on the founder entrepreneur. In some companies the founding father does still dominate the board even though he has long passed retiring age; in others the son or a professional manager has taken over and now he dominates the board.

At Point 3 we note certain defects in the accounting information systems. Sometimes only a glance is necessary to see that the board never look at the budgetary control figures or that they are constantly being taken by surprise by facts which, in most companies, would have been reported as a routine months before. There will be no updated cash flow forecast. If you ask them, for example, whether a certain figure is a marginal cost or a standard cost they will not know. But worse than that, at Point 4 we observe that although a major change has occurred no adequate response has been made. Perhaps two competitors have merged but the chief executive has decided 'it won't affect us'. Or the company has had its first strike which the board dismiss as being 'one of those things' when in fact it is a sign that they have lost touch with the shop floor.

It is well worth noting that these defects at Points 2, 3 and 4 are visible for months or years before the initial collapse occurs at Point 5. What happens at Point 5 is rather complex. Due to the various defects noted above the company will either overtrade or launch a big project which fails. Why should this happen? Because, having lost touch with their market or their customers or their employees right back at Point 4, almost anything they do may well go wrong. Also at Point 5 something else could happen; because we are dealing here with relatively large companies we have to recognize that pressure groups may impose such constraints that the company is damaged—and this could happen even if there are no defects, or relatively minor ones, at Points 2, 3 or 4. But another event can occur at Point 5: a normal business hazard. But if this occurred on its own, without either the overtrading or the project or the constraints, the consequences would certainly not be as severe as indicated by this massive collapse of the trajectory. Hazards occur continuously; they only cause severe damage like this when coincident with some other event. But overtrading and failed projects and constraints also occur without wreaking such havoc as the collapse here suggests. So what does happen at Point 5?

What I think happens is that at least two things go wrong together. An overtrade, a failed project, a constraint, or a hazard occur in any permutation of two or more. If only one of these occurs at Point 5 then the collapse does not take place—as I say, such things occur quite often and cause no more than a temporary setback to the normal healthy company. This is not a temporary setback. Nor is this a normal healthy company.

Following these events, profits fall severely at Point 6. At Point 7 the financial ratios deteriorate. At Point 8 morale falls and other non-financial symptoms appear. At Point 9 profits have still not recovered even though it may now be one or two years after Point 5. At Point 10 creative accounting begins, partly because the managers realize that they need a large loan. This, which is duly obtained at Point 11, lifts the gearing to dangerous levels. The company is now 'waterlogged'.

I use the term waterlogged to describe a company whose gearing is too high and which, *at the same time*, has lost its competitive edge. As we have seen (p. 135) a company whose gearing is too high has to pay such a large proportion of its profits straight out in interest charges that it has little left over to invest in the future. And a company which has lost its competitive edge will find it hard to make a successful product launch if they no longer fully understand the market or the needs of their customers. A company with both deficiencies at once is waterlogged—almost anything they do will send it to the bottom.

At Point 12, then, profits level out at last but at a volume that does little more than cover the interest payments. The general health of the company is 'poor' or a little above. Sales and profits are not going to bounce back on to a path of growth as a normal healthy company's would after a bad patch. I believe there are only a limited number of ways out for a waterlogged company. The first is to pay back some of the loans to the bank to reduce the gearing. But to do that the company would have to sell off assets or activities which would reduce the physical size of the company and such a move is alien to most managers. Another is to do nothing; but it only needs another wave, in the shape of another normal business hazard, and the vessel will sink.

The third is to improve profits so that the proportion paid out in interest is reduced and, eventually, the company can reduce the gearing, not by paying back the loan but by issuing more equity. Of course this is the way most companies select—indeed this is the normal process of corporate growth; where a company makes reasonable profits this allows a loan to be obtained which makes more profits which allows equity to be issued which later allows more loan and so on indefinitely. The fourth is to be taken over; not a solution that appeals to the man at the top of a company which has the defect we call one-man rule! Nor will he be attracted to another way out, liquidation; nor is there, at Point 12, any good reason to adopt that route, for the Type 3 trajectory does not necessarily imply that the company ever made a loss at Points 6 to 12—only that a severe drop in profit has occurred.

What in fact happens, I think, is that this type of company will invariably try to boost itself off the plateau—remember the Kariba power station, the RB 211 and the Penn Central merger. At Point 13, then, the managers will either launch a new ambitious project (a diversification perhaps, or a merger with a smaller company) or launch a campaign to expand sales from existing facilities. I suggest that whatever they do is doomed to failure; the project will fail and will break the company or the sales campaign will result in overtrading and will break the company. Why am I so sure that all attempts to boost off the plateau will fail? Because the gearing is so high and the company has so little cash to spare that *any* project that is big enough to get the company moving will be too big for its available resources. A small project would be safe but, of course, it would be too small to solve the problem. Also because they have lost touch with the market, the customers, the technology or whatever. Also because they will underestimate costs and overestimate revenues. Also because their accounting information is deficient and any calculations they make will be wrong, and they will be unaware of the fact until so late into the campaign or the project that corrective action cannot be effective. And because morale and self confidence is low. And because, having always in the past built a £2m factory each year they now do not appreciate that even a £1m factory is beyond their cash resources; yet now they will build one for £4m to boost the company out of trouble. At Point 14 sales and profits will rise due to these efforts and the apparent health of the company will improve—see the terminal hump on the trajectory. Everyone is relieved; the bank grants a loan or the shareholders subscribe for equity even though the net assets may already be negative. At Point 15 it will become clear that either the project is running into trouble or that sales are running ahead of the capital available to finance them, or a pressure group applies a constraint or a new normal business hazard appears. Or a permutation. Thus Point 15 is a repeat performance of Point 5—except that, in this case the company is already waterlogged. At Point 16 profits fail to cover interest payments, a cash flow crisis occurs and all the drama of the last few months begins. At Point 17 the Receiver is called in.

I am suggesting that mature companies go through three stages in their progress to failure. An initial collapse, a plateau, a final collapse. It seems to me highly unlikely that a mature company, which will undoubtedly have built up considerable reserves during its years or decades of profitable trading, can be struck down in one fell movement. Of course, I can imagine that the plateau from Point 12 to Point 15 might be only a month or two in duration; in that case the company might well appear to crash in one movement. But surely the probability of Point 15 following Point 5 so swiftly is very low bearing in mind how complex are the events at these points.

If I am right, and there is a lengthy period of plateau after the first collapse and before the final plunge, then a golden opportunity for rescue presents itself as will be described in the next chapter. I would not be surprised if the interval between Point 5 and Point 15 was four to five years—the period of the economic cycle—for many companies. For one of the normal business hazards that may strike at Points 5 and 15 is a credit squeeze or an economic recession. (If this is so, a company damaged in one recession may well be finished off in the next one. If so, bearing in mind the severity of the recession in 1974–5 all over the world, a considerable number of companies, injured then but not killed, will fail in 1978–80.) I cannot help noting again that the plateau in the case of Rolls-Royce was eight years, in Penn Central about 25, in British Leyland nearly a decade, in Alfred Herbert nearly a decade, in Mitchell Construction three years and Handley Page at least two.

In this description of the Type 3 trajectory I have tacitly assumed that the managers do not change during the whole process. A pattern of management succession always found in family business, and often elsewhere, is for the younger generation to take over from the old. This common pattern fits the Type 3 trajectory very well. I can imagine the old generation, having built up the company to its excellent condition at Point 1, now begins to grow old and to lose touch with the modern world (Points 3 and 4). The collapse, at Point 5, convinces the new generation that it is time for a change. Before they effect this, however, the company becomes waterlogged (Point 12). In their anxiety, enthusiasm or inexperience they try to boost the company off the plateau with the results we have already seen.

All companies are subject to normal business hazards and to constraints imposed by pressure groups and governments. All companies make mistakes—often very big ones like the Edsel and Project Intercept. Why are some companies thrown into insolvency by these while other companies are not? My answer is that when these events occur to Type 3 companies the consequences are severe because they are already weakened by certain defects—defects of management and accountancy and response to change, that a trained observer can often see. Not many people are looking for these, either inside or outside the company, but when all these damaging events and mistakes occur a second time, at Point 15, the consequences are fatal because now—and this *should* be obvious to everyone—the company is waterlogged as well.

It looks as though mature companies are given two lives, unlike Types 1 and 2 which can be felled with one blow. If this is so, it could have useful social implications for many of these companies are of some importance to the community in which they operate.

Only three trajectories?

So far as I know, no one has ever before suggested that failure conforms to a pattern, or rather, three patterns. At such an early stage in the systematic study of failure it would, I think, be a mistake to enter into greater detail or to try to generate more patterns than absolutely necessary. On the other hand, I do not wish to mislead by oversimplification. While refusing to admit that more than three trajectories are needed to explain the vast majority of failures that occur, I do feel bound to admit that a company following one trajectory could switch to another.

The most obvious occasion for a switch is the rescue of a company. Thus a Type 3 company, having suffered its intial collapse to Point 12 might be rescued and then live happily ever after as shown in Exhibit 8.5 Or a Type 2 might be rescued either before it becomes absurd at Point 14, say (see Exhibit 8.6), or on its way down after the peak (see Exhibit 8.7).

Alternatively an entirely healthy company could be taken over by a manager of unusual ambition who, in his attempt to achieve fame and fortune breaks the company. This happens quite often to very small companies which are used as 'a shell' by an entrepreneur, as was probably the case in Wilstar Securities (p. 25). While it seldom happens to a very large company, I believe it did happen to Burmah Oil from 1968 to 1974. Burmah was a perfectly normal company until the early sixties when its management decided upon a strategy of diversification. But in 1968 Mr Nick Williams began to accelerate this process so that in 1974 Burmah took over Signal Oil Company. At that time Burmah's total capitalization was £1000m of which £600m was equity and £400m loan. But to buy Signal, Burmah borrowed a further £180m, thus increasing its gearing to 50 per cent. Within months of this purchase the world economy turned down and the UK government had to go to Burmah's rescue. This story, more akin to a Type 2 failure than a mature Type 3, occurs more frequently to smaller companies and, I suggest, consists of a switch in trajectory from a non-failing trajectory to a Type 2, as shown in Exhibit 8.8.

Presumably any change from one style of top management to another,

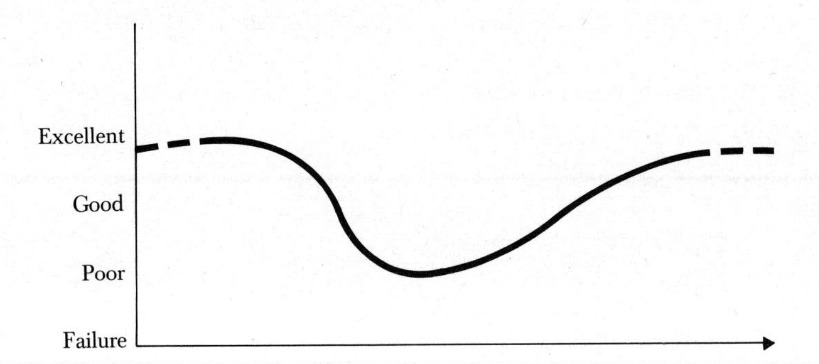

Exhibit 8.5. Rescue of a Type 3 company after its initial collapse has occurred

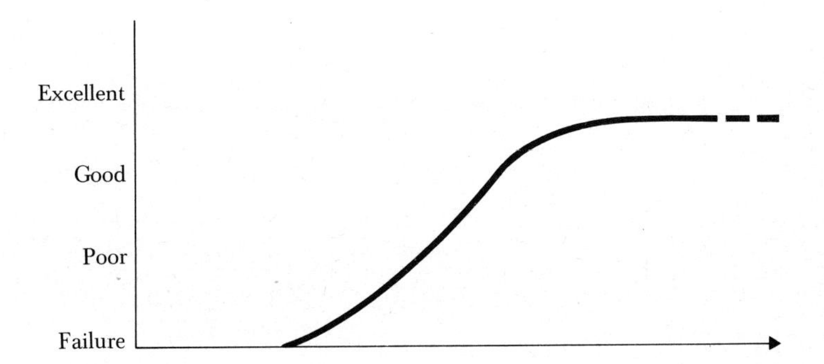

Exhibit 8.6. Rescue of a Type 2 company before the peak has been reached

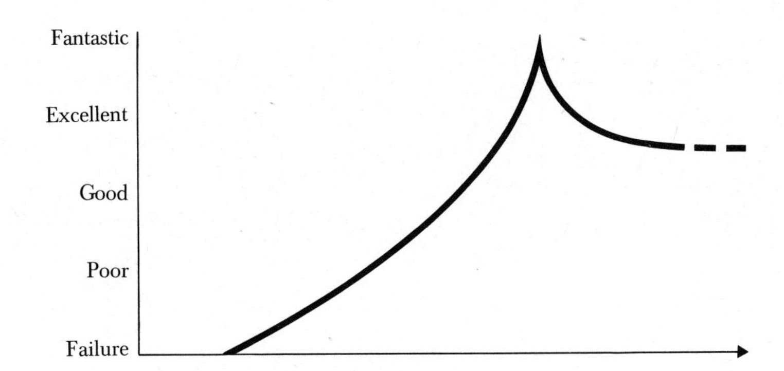

Exhibit 8.7. Rescue of a Type 2 company after the peak has been reached

whether caused by retirement or a palace revolution or by a shareholder group or a government, can cause a switch from one trajectory to another. I believe that a change of management is, in fact, the only thing that can switch a company from one failure trajectory to another. Perhaps one should go further and suggest that if a change in top management occurs the interested observer should *expect* a switch in trajectory.

I wish to end this chapter by repeating a warning made before. The world is a complex place full of variety. In this whirling kaleidoscope it would be odd, to say the least, if there were only three ways in which

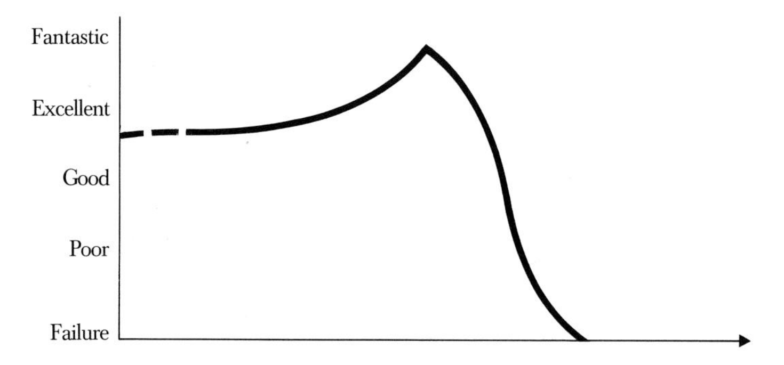

Exhibit 8.8. A switch from a non-failing trajectory into a Type 2 failure trajectory

companies could fail. It would be odd, if, with clockwork regularity, we were able to predict that a company displaying this defect will fail only in this manner while another company displaying some other defect can only slide down some other strictly grooved passage. I believe that as one identifies more and more of the points and as a suspect company travels further and further down one of my trajectories, one's anxiety should mount. Perhaps it should become so acute that, whether the company would have failed or not, one should intervene.

Of course, on the other hand, many will fail without ever displaying any of the signs at all and never having moved down any of the three trajectories.

9. *Prevention and cure*

I believe we now know a very great deal more about corporate collapse than we did when we started. We know that a company which exhibits a particular defect of top management structure may also exhibit other defects. If we find these we know that it will have a propensity to make certain mistakes. We know that if it makes them certain symptoms may appear. We know that if they do then the future course of the failure may follow a certain path. Thus we have at least a rudimentary knowledge of the pathogenesis of failure, its diagnosis and its prognosis. We even know the diathesis, or tendency, of three different types of company to fail in three very different ways. Now the question is: do we know enough to be able to prevent failure or to cure companies once they have started to move down their failure path? Can we, for example, put into the hands of those currently useless outside directors and bank representatives enough knowledge to allow them to do their job?

I think we can. But first I must ask a simple question. Do we *want* to prevent or cure failure? Or, on the contrary, should we be aiming to *increase* the failure rate? The question has to be asked since the concept of capitalism includes Darwin's rule of survival of the fittest. In the capitalist system the resources of society are transferred from one application to another, deemed to be more useful, by the decline and failure of companies that are not using resources usefully and by the rise and success of companies that are. If we tamper with this mechanism by reducing the number of failures, are we not going to damage the efficiency of capitalism?

I believe that is a real danger. Many people believe that the system has already been damaged by the monopolistic powers of big companies on the one hand, and of trade unions on the other. Some companies are now so large that they are virtually indestructible and, however incompetently or inappropriately they are using the community's resources, their failure cannot be brought about. The trade unions, by insisting upon job security, even more effectively prevent the movement of resources to new needs. Let us not add to these awesome forces of waste by postponing the failure of companies which deserve to fail. On the other hand, just as some companies which should fail do not do so, other companies which are weeded out by the principle of survival of the fittest, ought possibly not to have been—was Rolls-Royce a weed? Or they fail in a manner that is damaging to society—if Penn Central had been allowed to fail it would have caused enormous hardship to employees, suppliers and customers and threatened the entire social fabric of a dozen States.

What I think we should try to do with our new-found knowledge is not to use it to prevent all failures blindly, nor mindlessly to increase them, but to use it to *regulate* failure. More of some, less of others, slowing the process here, speeding it there, in order to improve the efficiency of capitalism as a means of allocating the resources of society but with due attention to possible consequential hardship and harm to vulnerable members of society.

In the sections which follow I shall discuss a number of measures that may be useful in achieving this aim. As we already recognize three quite different types of company, each of which happens to have a different rôle in society, I will divide these comments into the three convenient categories with which we are already familiar.

Type 1. Prevention and cure

Type 1 companies are nearly always very small. While these failures must collectively be of some social consequence—there are a great number of them each year—my view is that our concern should be for the proprietor rather than for society in this case. When a Type 1 company fails it is he who usually loses most because, as it never got off the ground, very few other people are deeply dependent upon it.

Let us first consider the possibility of cure. Can anything be done to save the company, or a worthwhile part of it, once it begins to fail? I think not. Remember that it fails, usually, because the proprietor has very seriously overestimated the revenues or underestimated the costs of his project. Not just by a fraction, by a whole world. By the time he discovers his mistake I believe it is always too late to arrange a takeover or to cut back or economize or boost sales significantly. Remember also that, except for a very considerable knowledge of the product itself, he lacks many of the skills required for business today. (And today one has to be good to survive; to succeed one has to be superb.) Type 1 companies also have high gearing; it gets higher as insolvency approaches. The only Type 1 defect that can be cured is the accountancy information system but curing that cannot save the company. It is said that prevention is better than cure; in this case it certainly is, for as a general rule, Type 1 failures cannot be cured. Even if they could the cost of the salaries of skilled accountants and others in doing so might far outweigh the value of the company, bearing in mind how small the profitable core would be.

If a cure cannot be effected then, it seems to me, a policy of euthanasia —or in this case infanticide—is indicated. I believe that in the case of many Type 1 failures it becomes clear very early on in the trajectory that the company will always be a weakling, vulnerable to the next normal business hazard that occurs. An opinion on its probable viability can be formed at Point 5, which may be years before the company would normally fail at Point 13. Between Points 5 and 13 resources are being wasted, the creditors are progressively bearing the losses (although they do not know this) and the proprietor himself will be suffering all the mental and financial agonies associated with failure. But if this euthanasia argument is valid, who should step in and persuade the proprietor to give up? The answer is simple: it should be the bank.

If the banks are to play a larger rôle as a source of capital for business in Britain—and see the rapidly rising figures shown on p. 43 and note the much greater rôle of banks on the Continent—then a major review of their policies is required. I do not think it is an exaggeration to say that these are at present wholly inadequate. When an intending entrepreneur approaches his bank for a loan to start a company the bank's concern is less for the probable viability of the company than for collateral. The bank is more interested in whether his house is worth more than the loan, than whether his business has the slightest chance of success. As the banks are already, I believe, the most important regulator in the success or failure of Type 1 companies, a less negative attitude to their clients seems indicated. As for the banks standing back with arms folded until the company's decline threatens their loan—a policy noted by many of the experts—I find it difficult to understand, for by then the company is lost beyond recall.

When a proprietor applies for a loan that is more than trivial in amount, I believe the banks should play a more active rôle. Thus a bank could substantially reduce the incidence of failure by ensuring that potential Type 1 companies are never launched. We know the defects from which they usually suffer even before they begin, and it only requires a bank representative to sit down with the proprietor and draw up a budget for the proposed company, together with a cash flow plan, and to perform a sensitivity test (see p. 181) on the key figures, to determine whether the company has the slightest chance of success. If it has not, the loan should not be granted. If it has, and the loan is granted, then these calculations may be referred to again every six months, say, and progress judged. If it becomes clear that the project has been severely miscalculated—i.e., that Point 5 has been reached—then the sooner the bank forecloses the better, especially if, as Altman reminds us, an economic recession is in prospect.

Such a policy by the banks would achieve three improvements. It would prevent a number of Type 1 companies ever being launched. It would bring them to a merciful end as soon as an incontrovertible diagnosis of impending failure was made. It would allow much larger loans to be made to companies that are not obvious Type 1 failure candidates, thus increasing the number and quality of viable small companies. I believe that a society dominated by large companies is substantially less attractive to live in than one in which a great number of small companies are allowed to operate. But not if many of them are weaklings. The banks bear a considerable measure of responsibility in regulating this feature of a nation's life.

Type 2. Prevention and cure

A completely different situation confronts us with Type 2 company failures.

For one thing, they grow so large that a great number of people other than the proprietor become dependent upon them. For another, there is usually a profitable core that is well worth salvaging even after insolvency. From society's point of view, and even from the proprietor's, the correct moment for intervention is after Points 8, 9 or 10—by which stage a diagnosis and prognosis can be made with some confidence—but before Points 12, 13 and 14 when the rapid collapse becomes inevitable.

I can see no case for intervention by anyone in the early sections of the trajectory. Better to leave the launch and period of rapid growth to the entrepreneur entirely. Few people have the ability to assist or guide such men even if they would accept advice, which few of them do. But it is not long before several dozen—or even several thousand—people become dependent upon the company for employment or insurance or holidays or loans or housing or whatever. In view of the fact that society now believes that profitmaking organizations may make profits only if they harm no one in the process, some form of control will have to be imposed whenever any company grows to become socially important.

Long before the entrepreneur does his Samson act at Points 14 or 15, therefore, some measure of regulation must be imposed upon him by those who will be harmed when he brings the temple down. Nothing significant would be lost even if, in attempting to gain control over him, he resigned in anger, for his wealth and the company itself would be intact which neither might be if he remained until Points 12 to 15. Of course, if control can be obtained without the founder of the company leaving in a huff, so very much the better. How might this be achieved?

I think it is worth considering the various possible power structures that might be invoked in the case of Type 2 companies in some detail, for these may also be employed in all companies that grow to become socially significant. The key cause of failure is one-man rule. When one man dominates a company he confers upon it a singleminded purpose which, if he is right, leads to outstanding success but, if he is wrong, leads to failure. No man is infallible. Eventually all one-man rules *must* fail, whether they are Type 1 or Type 2 or Type 3. What we should seek to do, then, is to allow the one man full rein when he is right but hold him in when he is wrong. Of course, we do not know when he is going to be wrong but we can give him full rein until he has built up a socially significant organization and then, whether he will go on being right or not, rein him in. We have to bottle the genie.

I find it quite remarkable that so little thought has been given to this aspect of organization structure—the only new idea under consideration is the supervisory board, a sledgehammer device. And yet, since the decline of the shareholder, decades ago now, a great vacuum of power exists above the chief executive. I believe there are a number of ways in which some form of control may be gained over chief executives, some of which I list below in order of application by size of company.

1. In the case of very small companies, a measure of control may be obtained whenever a bank lends the company money (above trivial amounts). As described above (p. 172) all that is needed is for the bank to make budget and cash flow calculations and to monitor the company's progress against these every few months.
2. As the size of the loans and the company grow the bank will need to place a representative on the board. He should not be paid solely by the company, as is the current practice, but partly at least by the bank. He should be briefed to do nothing and say nothing other than what is necessary to satisfy himself that the company is not moving on to a failure trajectory. He should be expert in this task.
3. Alternatively, as above but not on the board. All he needs is sufficient access to the company to do his job.
4. As the loans grow, the bank should consider taking an equity stake proportional to the loans. Or develop close links with, and perhaps share a representative on the board with, any large shareholders other than the proprietor.
5. Other groups of stakeholders (i.e., any one who now has a significant stake in the success or failure of the company, such as employees, suppliers, customers, the local community) should begin to share this representative as they become more dependent upon the company. It may worth noting that normally all these groups have completely different and irreconcilable objectives: some want more pay, others cheaper goods, others more dividends. But in one thing they can unite and be represented by one man—none of them want the company to fail.
6. Leach makes the statement (p. 32) that managers' risk-taking flair is damaged when they are subjected to supervision. Leaving aside the comment that, after a certain point society *wants* the managers of a large company to take fewer risks, we have to accept his implied principle that supervision should be kept down to the essential

minimum. I believe this precludes using the law to enforce the right of stakeholder representation until it is unavoidable. Thus, while it might be technically possible to enact a law that, for example, gives the local community the right to a seat on the board of a company employing more than five per cent of the local population, this should be avoided. But it might be possible to set up a more flexible legal mechanism, such as a tribunal, empowered to order a company to accept a board representative from any group of stakeholders who convince the tribunal that they would be severely affected by the failure of their company.

7. As a company increases still further in size, having now perhaps several hundred employees, a single director representing the banks and other stakeholders may prove insufficient. It may then be time for them to appoint an independent chairman whose duty is not to supplement the chief executive in the management of the company, but to ensure that the interests of the shareholders, the banks, the stakeholders (and society in general if the company is large) are clearly stated and adquately safeguarded in whatever the company does.
8. Finally we come to the supervisory board which, as Leach also notes, has the very severe disadvantage that no society has sufficient resources of intelligent, incorruptible people to staff more than a few such boards. There are other most severe disadvantages but it may be that the tide of public opinion is so strong that large companies will be forced to accept these boards.

I have dealt at some length with methods of intervention at this particular juncture—where we are concerned with Type 2—because of all companies this is the one with the most autocratic chief executive and where the mistakes of one man can most extensively be visited upon others. Unless the Type 2 chief executive is subject to some measure of control no means will be found at any point in the entire trajectory, from start to end, either to prevent or to cure failure. If the genie can be bottled, however, both prevention—at around Points 8 to 11—and cure—from Point 12 onwards—may be effective. Prevention may take the form of constraining the chief executive's excesses of enthusiasm. Cure may take the form of cutting back or selling off any unprofitable activities, probably those that the entrepreneur launched shortly before the collapse. Or a takeover may be arranged. Or whatever. But whatever the cure, it is almost certainly not something that the entrepreneur would have contemplated himself. Cutting back? Selling off? A merger? I hardly think so! Once again I think we see that prevention is better than cure. Both are possible, but the cure involves loss of jobs or money or something for a number of people.

Let me summarize this section. If we leave it to the entrepreneur, he will not only launch his company successfully and bring to the market place some new and often exciting product or service but he will build a large vibrant organization in a matter of a few hectic years. But it will then crash to the ground, for these men do not know when to stop. When it crashes down a great number of people may be hurt. But this can be prevented if, as the company grows, a progressively greater measure of control over his excesses is obtained by banks, shareholders, stakeholders and the community. The means to do this exist. If they are used, these Type 2 companies may be diverted out of their failure trajectory into a non-failing trajectory to the great benefit of all concerned. In other words, the criterion and justification for intervention in a private or a public company's affairs is not whether it is well or badly managed, nor whether it is a success or a failure, but whether it is socially significant.

Type 3. Prevention and cure

Again the problem is different. Here we have a mature company, often a large or medium-sized one upon which a number of people have already become dependent. Both prevention and cure are possible; cure is possible along almost the whole length of the very long trajectory. What should be our attitude to these companies?

I believe we should try to prevent their failure, certainly, but much more important, should not allow them to remain waterlogged for years. In that condition they are using resources inefficiently and causing concern to all. As soon as Point 12 is reached, then, the banks or shareholders or younger managers or stakeholders or government should insist upon a fundamental change of management together with a severe but controlled retrenchment or the sale of unprofitable activities or of property or other assets. Or seek to be taken over. Let us recall Altman's remarks (p. 67) that whatever is done has to be something more than mere cosmetics. It will certainly include a capital restructure and, probably, the repayment of loans to reduce gearing. All this is painful and none of it will be done if the company is controlled either by the old top management or by its employees, some of whom, of course, must lose their jobs. It is in circumstances such as these that the composition of a supervisory board, the voting power of an independent chairman, and the power of a bank representative against the shareholder representative against the employee's representative, really matter. I said above that much thought needs to be given to these dispositions of power.

If these dispositions allow a radical change to be made then:

1. Virtually the whole of the top management may have to be changed.
2. The gearing will have to be very substantially cut back.
3. If the company has been overtrading, then, since much of the recently acquired business will probably be at low margins, a severe cutback in volume may be needed.
4. If the company has recently launched a big project, this may have to be abandoned or sold.

Action postponed after Point 12 will only result in more severe action being needed later on by the Receiver. I realize that all such cures are painful but I find it incredible that no one felt able, during the whole decade that it was waterlogged, to put Rolls-Royce right; nor British Leyland, nor Alfred Herbert, nor Penn Central.

Turning now to prevention of Type 3 failures, we are hampered by the same problem as in Type 2. If an autocrat is in control of the company, nothing can be done without his consent. One of the things we want to do is to dismiss him or reduce his power. He will not be enthusiastic. Either this defect is going to be put right before Point 5, or after it, when the company will be sadly weakened, or after Point 15, when it will be insolvent. I believe that someone has to take their courage in both hands and challenge the right of one man to dominate a company upon which a great number of people have become dependent. Of course, if everyone has great confidence in him, if his board is not unbalanced, if his finance function is well represented, if his accountancy information systems are in excellent shape, if the company responds eagerly to change, well then, no action is needed. But clearly this company is not displaying a sufficient number of the causes listed in chapter 7 to be classified as a Type 3—it is a non-failing company.

Where there are grounds for concern, then, someone has to act. I believe the best agent is again the bank or banks. Let them initiate one of the measures for supervising chief executives listed above (p. 174). Of all the parties interested in the welfare of the company, the banks are most skilled in the delicate task of intervention at this level of seniority. Let them discreetly intervene, let them set up a supervisory board or appoint a chairman or dismiss the chief executive or even the whole board. Then let them ensure that someone introduces three more corrective measures: one is to put right any other of the six defects in management structure we have come to associate with one-man rule. Another is to correct any defects in the accounting information system. The third is to introduce corporate planning. While I am not convinced that corporate planning is desirable in many of the Type 1 or Type 2 companies, which are often too small and too entrepreneurial respectively to warrant it, I am totally convinced of its necessity in mature companies of *any* size (except perhaps the one-man band).

The value of corporate planning is threefold. First, it helps to sort out what each group of stakeholders want from the company. The shareholders want dividends and capital gains; but how much of each and what else do they want? What do the employees want? Must a company inevitably aim to grow in physical size or is it legitimate to remain at some optimum size instead? Should a minimum acceptable profit target be set so that managers know how well they *must* perform as well as setting them the usual challenging target? How should the company behave in society today? The systematic approach to these crucial modern questions characterizes the early stages of the corporate planning process. Then, second, the process moves on to identifying relevant long-term changes in the environment of the company and to selecting suitable strategic responses—exactly the sort of activity which, when left undone as it often is in Type 3 companies, leads to collapse at Point 5. Third, corporate planning provides for the continuous systematic monitoring of the company's position in the world as it is and as it is expected to become, so that adequate warning of trouble ahead may be given to the board.

Corporate planning can thus be of inestimable value not only in reducing the chances of failure but in shaping the company into a strategic structure designed to take advantage of opportunities as they appear. But it is a tool strictly for use by the top team of a company; we will not see many companies using it where the top team is dominated by one man. And an unbalanced board composed, for example, of engineers is not likely to use a tool that depends for its effectiveness on the participation of accountants, finance men, marketing and purchasing managers. And no board with a weak finance function will adopt corporate planning, for although corporate planning is not predominantly a finance tool, nevertheless finance is its keystone.

I would like to repeat a comment made before. The reason I am suggesting that banks or groups of outsiders should intervene in the affairs of a company in which they are deemed to have a stake is that today this is dictated by the prevailing mood of society. I am suggesting that, in conformity with this viewpoint, the social penalty for not intervening in a suspect company which then fails is often greater than intervening in a suspect company which might not have failed if it had been left alone.

Whether one welcomes this trend or not is irrelevant; this is how the world is. I only hope that our examination of failure here will help to reduce the number of interventions made unnecessarily, while making those that are necessary more timely and more effective. If it must be done, let it be done well.

The company survival kit

I shall briefly summarize here the minimum measures that companies should take. Unlike the advice to managers found in most textbooks this is not a recipe for achieving success; it is one for avoiding failure.

First, the *top management*. When starting a business, avoid taking into partnership only people with the same knowledge as yourself—a top team composed of all talents helps to ensure that none of the complexities of the modern world outwits you. Indeed, any unbalanced top team in any company is a clear warning of trouble in store. In particular, not surprisingly since business is about money and the creation of wealth, take a strong finance man into the top team. Avoid putting people on the board who do nothing, say nothing, know nothing and do not even care. Avoid creating a gap in management ability below board level—there must be management in depth.

Above all, make sure that when a company grows beyond a certain point—the rules for identifying it are not known but it is nevertheless recognizable—make sure that one-man rule is gradually diluted. Or that an autocrat is supervised by someone who represents the interests of people not in the executive hierarchy but outside the company—shareholders or banks or customers or the community. Many supervisory devices are possible, including the rather clumsy supervisory board which is suitable only for enormous companies. An independent chairman is an excellent concept; that his rôle is wholly different to that of a chief executive must be understood clearly.

Second, the *accountancy information.* Do budgets, cash flows, costings. Budgets can be quite simple and are well within the ability of any person who runs a business. But they are quite useless unless, every few weeks—usually every four—an 'actual' figure is calculated and compared with the budget. The same remarks apply to cash flow calculations: 'If they are not updated they are useless; if they are, they are invaluable', said Curtis. Given these two vital forecasting, planning and control documents, a number of very useful management ratios can be derived from them, including Altman's Z, to monitor the company's propensity to failure. This is an appropriate moment to return to a slogan I used in chapter 1. I said then that it is as much a part of a manager's task to avoid failure as it is to achieve success. One practical manifestation of a management's realization of this philosophy would be if they monitored those financial ratios (including Z) that would warn them of possible failure—a watch that few managers keep—as well as monitoring their progress towards a challenging target—a watch that most good managers today already keep.

Not to know what a product costs to produce may well lead to expensive mistakes. But this figure may not be the same as the marginal cost or the opportunity cost or the full standard cost. If the top team are not at home with these terms—if, for example, they are not familiar with contribution analysis—it is difficult to see how they can avoid making serious mistakes in pricing products, in launching projects, in shifting resources from one part of the company to another, in closing down activities, in calculating savings from a merger—and a hundred other decisions.

Third, the *response to change.* Adopt a systematic corporate planning procedure. This means identifying what the company's long-term objectives are. Then examine the company to list its major strengths and weaknesses—i.e., what it is really good at or bad at. Then forecast what trends and events in the future environment of the company are likely to be important. Then devise a long-term strategy which will carry the company forward in a shape and condition that allows it to take advantage of opportunities and avoid threats. Finally set up a long-term strategy monitoring system.

One of the areas of long-term change that are scrutinized in most systematic systems of corporate planning (including, of course, the one I devised) is the trend in constraints imposed on companies by society. A company neglects this at its peril.

Fourth, look to your *gearing*. Once a company's gearing rises to a certain level it becomes vulnerable to normal business hazards. One never knows when these will occur—usually they do so with fiendish perversity just when one's gearing is at a peak. The only advice is never to allow loan interest to reach a level at which the company's cash flow is threatened if a normal business hazard does occur. (One cannot legislate for bad luck, however. Bad luck is one or more normal business hazards of such severity or in such rapid succession, that no one would expect you to take account of them in the management of the company. An 'abnormal business hazard', if you like.)

One useful tool in determining a prudent level of gearing is the cash flow forecast plus sensitivity test. Briefly: one takes a normal cash flow calculation based on the most reasonable assumptions that one can make as to interest rates, profits and so on. Then one alters these assumptions to calculate how sensitive these cash flows are to these changed assumptions. What would happen if interest rates doubled towards the end of the year? Or if profits were halved? Or if a strike postpones the start-up of a new plant? When one has completed a number of these tests it may emerge that, in each case, the cash flows are dangerously curtailed—that is a useful warning that the gearing used in the calculations is too high.

Fifth. *Avoid overtrading*. Entrepreneurs, proprietors and managers all have one thing in common—they worship growth, expansion, size, big numbers, empires. No manager goes home and boasts to his wife that he has been put in charge of an even smaller project than his last one. Be warned: if an ambitious target in terms of turnover or sales units or share of the market is given to a department or to a manager, without being linked to an equally ambitious target for profits or profit margins, then the company is in severe danger of overtrading.

Sixth. *Avoid the big project*. Here I can only quote Cork's law: Do not enter into any obligation that you may not be able to meet. Few managers would be so foolish as to launch a project that is so big *at the time it is launched* that it will bring down the company. That is not usually the problem. The problem is that costs become so much higher and revenues so much less than originally envisaged that this brings the company down.

I suggest a sensitivity test again. Make the usual project appraisal calculations based on reasonable assumptions as to costs, revenues and time schedules. Then, altering each major assumption in turn, calculate how bad it has to be before it brings down the company. Then judge whether it can possibly get that bad. If it could, do not undertake the project under any circumstances whatever.

Let us learn a lesson from Rolls-Royce. When it undertook the RB 211-22 (not to be confused with the earlier RB 211 project) it estimated the R&D costs at £90m. Eventually they rose to over £200m. That ratio is 2·2 but, as the Inspectors say, 'no one . . . can plausibly claim to be surprised' because R&D costs on high technology projects often treble or more. When selecting 'worst case' assumptions for sensitivity tests, then, look back at similar projects to see how wrong you were with them. If you have not done one like this before be doubly careful.

I hope these hints in this 'survival kit' will help companies to avoid the major errors associated with failure; these are management defects, accountancy information defects, lack of response to change, high gearing, overtrading and the big project. I do not wish to labour the point but the philosophy behind this book is that managers are as much responsible for avoiding failure as for achieving success—perhaps more so in view of the terrible consequences of failure compared with the pleasant but ephemeral fruits of success. To set a challenging target, to devise a strategy to achieve it and to monitor progress towards it is now a routine of good management. To set a *minimum acceptable* target, to devise a strategy to ensure it will be *exceeded* and to monitor that one's company is *not failing* is, I believe, the urgent new criterion of good management.

What a government can do

A number of actions by governments seem to be indicated by what we have learnt. Some are relatively minor adjustments to the law. It seems inappropriate, for example, that a person convicted of fraud should be permitted to form a company. A view occasionally expressed is that company directors should be granted a licence to practise as directors, which could be withheld temporarily or permanently for certain misdemeanours. And it is strange that a person may form a company, put it into liquidation, watch the creditors pay his company's debts and then, perhaps after a holiday abroad, do it all over again. One would think that some alterations to limited liability laws are overdue; one suggestion is that limited liability status should be withdrawn from certain companies for certain misdemeanours. Another is that companies should pay a percentage of their profits into a bankruptcy bond from which the stakeholders (but not the shareholders, of course) would be compensated in case of failure.

There is also the problem of disclosure. All over the world companies are being made to disclose more figures, more decisions, more forecasts and plans. In some nations more has to be disclosed to the employees than to the shareholders. I have heard it suggested that the press should attend board meetings—the national press would attend the meetings of large companies, the local press of smaller ones. What, one wonders, will be the effect of more disclosure being required from companies that are failing? I suggest there may be two opposing consequences. The managers of some companies will remain so utterly determined that no one shall know they are failing that they will employ even greater cunning and indulge in even more devious creative accounting. This will lead, as we have seen, to even more sudden and severe failure. But other managers of failing companies will abide by the law and the true state of their companies will be known earlier, thus enabling more satisfactory rescues to be made. I am inclined to believe that greater disclosure will be greeted on balance by greater cunning, and therefore by an increase in sudden, severe failures. Entrepreneurs are very tenacious.

Parallel with this move to greater disclosure is the tightening of the law on insider trading. I find myself in two minds about this also. Perhaps my views are coloured by the thought of Saunders losing $750 000 because he felt he ought not to sell his Penn Central shares when the company was ailing, while apparently Bevan, who did sell his, made a profit of $400 000. My two opposing opinions are that unless the law on insider trading is tightened, managers with inside knowledge of a company will continue to take advantage of those without it; but on the other hand, I cannot reconcile this trend in legislation with the need to rescue failing companies. If, instead of placing further restraints on insider trading, these were reduced, then the share price of a company would more closely reflect the confidence of its senior managers. Thus everyone would know how well it was doing and when it was not doing so well. Sudden and severe collapses would thus take place less often and more rescues could be effected.

I cannot avoid concluding that, if it is desirable to expose a company's true position to all who are concerned to know—and I think it is—then more disclosure will help but little, unless accompanied by *more* freedom for insider trading, not less. So long as legislation continues to move in opposite directions I see nothing but more subterfuge and more confusion and fewer rescues. The above comments do not take account of the fact that many senior managers receive shares in their company as part of their normal remuneration; it may be asking too much of many of these human beings to expect them not to sell out when they lose confidence in the future of their company.

The merit in everyone knowing how well a company is really doing—as opposed to how well it says it is—is that the last few months, with all their swift uncontrollable drama, may be avoided and an orderly rescue may be mounted. It would be of great assistance if national governments were to develop coherent policies on the provision of loans or guarantees for loans while these rescues were being made. But even where such rescues are possible, a considerable number of employees, suppliers or customers may need support because, almost invariably, a rescue means surgery. Another action required by government, then, is to develop a coherent policy towards groups of people injured by failure and rescue. Opposition to cutting back a failing company's activities usually stems from people who are likely to suffer, but no coherent policy setting out the extent and, more important, the limits, of such aid exists. The story of Penn Central might have been very different if, instead of forcing the company to accommodate the every wish of every protesting party, the US government had offered them some form of compensation. They would then, no doubt, have gone away and found something useful to do instead of remaining to leech the life blood of the company!

Another world-wide trend is the move towards the closer supervision of companies by supra-executive devices such as supervisory boards. While most people accept that companies should be more accountable to society there is less agreement upon the best instrument. I dislike the supervisory boards as being excessively cumbersome, quite apart from Leach's point about staffing them. I prefer an independent chairman, a sort of one-man supervisory board, which obviates Leach's objection. But what causes me greater anxiety is the trend towards legislating these devices on to companies. The law is a blunt instrument. It results in such anomalies as a company employing 1999 people not having to have a supervisory board while one employing 2000 does have to.

I would prefer to see a tribunal to which any group of people could apply to obtain supervisory powers over any company in which they could demonstrate an interest. The decision of the tribunal would rest mainly upon how severely the applicants would be harmed if the company were to fail. The form that this supervision would take—an independent chairman, a supervisory board or whatever—would depend upon the size of the company and many other factors which a tribunal could take into account but which legislation could not.

Finally, governments can affect company failure by vacillation. They do not even appear capable of deciding whether they want companies to make profits or not. The US government apparently wanted to see the Penn Central merger take place and, at the same time, clearly did not want it. But let us not waste words on this; governments have forever turned their coats and presumably always will. I wish I did not feel that they keep on getting worse and worse.

What the banks can do

It seems to me that the banks came out of this study rather badly. They were accused of 'generosity' by one expert. Another noted how they were 'caught with their wallets exposed'. One of the writers noted repeatedly how the banks and financial institutions were continually being caught out.

In a nutshell, I believe the problem is that the banks base their loan policy on the assumption that they will be able to identify a failing company and extract their loans before its asset value falls below the value of those loans. It is quite clear that, too often, they cannot. So abysmal are they at this task that they even go on lending to companies in their last few months—see Rolls-Royce, Penn Central and Nihon Netsugaku Kogyo (p. 25).

I believe that this difficulty is soluble. Two elements in the solution are of overwhelming importance: one is the existence of a technology of failure prediction, the other is an administrative mechanism for applying this technology. I hope that this book provides the former, perhaps for the first time. I have made a number of suggestions as to the latter (on p. 174) and it is my view that, for any given company and any given size of loan, one of these mechanisms is preferable to another and the criteria for choice are clear. It is no more than common sense that for a large loan to a small company a bank would need much closer control (perhaps by appointing the company's chairman) than for a similar loan to a large company (where a part-time representative is probably sufficient).

But standing firmly in the way of any solution is an inexcusable confusion of mind over the rôle of outside directors. A company appoints outside directors for any of several excellent reasons. Perhaps they need close contact with a particular sectional interest—such as the cotton industry or farmers or Brazilian coffee planters—and so they appoint a suitable person as a liaison at board level. Or they need occasional access to a highly skilled specialist—in electronics or economics or virus infections—and appoint him at board level because he is so eminent in his field they can hardly do anything else. Or they wish to bring influence to bear on some group of people who can be useful to them so they appoint an outstanding member of that group—a member of parliament, a banker, a trade unionist—whose task is to influence government policy or improve their prospects for loans or contain union militancy.

It will be noted that all these rather different outside directors have one thing in common: they are appointed by and paid by the company and they work for its management in the furtherance of the company's prosperity. Now this relationship seems to me wholly different, not just in degree but in kind, to the relationship of the representative of a bank which has lent money to the company. The rôle of this type of outside director is to ensure that the loan is safe and to run at high speed to the bank if he thinks it is not.

He is not there to further the prosperity of the company; he is not there to give advice on finance or any other topic; he is not there to bring pressure to bear on influential groups. Of course, he may do all these things (I hope he does), but that is not his job. His job is to warn the bank—one assumes after repeated warnings to his board colleagues first—that the company is not being managed in such a way that the loan will continue to be safe (or, of course, that no further loans should be granted, or to make comments on other aspects of loan policy). Now this man should be appointed by the bank (with the approval of the company), paid by the bank (or partially by the company) and work for the bank (while being helpful towards the company).

I believe this is a most delicate job and I therefore suggested, on p. 174, that perhaps the bank representative ought not to be on the board at all. Properly briefed, armed with new knowledge of failure, this man could be effective. He could become a professional bank representative for a number of their clients. But he could also become something else—a representative for other groups of people who also want to be sure that the company is not going to fail, such as the shareholders, employees, local community, creditors. They all have this in common—that they do not want their company to fail—while in all other matters their aims and needs and beliefs are totally different and sometimes irreconcilable. One signal advantage for all these groups sharing the bank's representative is that he is likely to be unbiased, incorruptible and highly competent.

What the stakeholders can do

Half a century ago, most company chief executives recognized one and only one group of people as their boss—the shareholders. As their influence declined (collapsed would be a better word) the influence of all the other stakeholders increased but no one single coherent group—such as all the creditors or all the employees or all the customers—arose to fill the power vacuum. What happened was that the chief executive played the rôles of both chief manager and chairman. One-man rule is a major element in failure; even if it did not so often lead to failure it is still a danger *wherever* it occurs—as the American Presidency in 1973–4 exemplified.

In my view, the only action that stakeholders need take is to ensure that their company has a competent chairman as well as a chief executive. Neglect that and nothing can protect them; attend to it and failure becomes improbable.

I also believe that, once a company is built up by its founder to a size that casts its shadow over the lives of a significant number of people, these people have a right to a voice, not in the *management* of the company —that is a lunatic proposal made by people who do not know how skilled managers must be today—but in its behaviour as it affects their lives. They ought to be able to stop it from causing significant harm to them, they ought to be able to make their views known to it. At present this is possible, but only intermittently and often in anger. No mechanism exists.

The supervisory board is one mechanism. An independent chairman is another. I believe that until we develop these, or some alternative systematic channels of communication, the full potential of our companies to create wealth without causing harm will never be realized. Worse, so shrill and sometimes vicious do the various stakeholders now become in their frustrated attempt to make their voices heard by their company, that it is brought to failure.

Bibliography

Altman, Edward I., *Corporate Bankruptcy in America*, Heath Lexington Books, 1971.

Barmash, Isadore, *Great Business Disasters*, Ballantine Books, 1973.

Birchfield, Reg, *The Rise and Fall of JBL*, NBR Books, 1972.

Brooks, John, *The Fate of the Edsel*, Gollancz, 1964.

Daughen, J. R. and P. Binzen, *The Wreck of the Penn Central*, Little, Brown and Company, 1971.

Deeson, A. F. L., *Great Company Crashes*, W. Foulsham, 1972.

Department of Trade, *Report on International Learning Systems*, HMSO, 1971.

Department of Trade, *Rolls-Royce Limited*, HMSO, 1973.

Robertson, Andrew, *The Lessons of Failure*, Macdonald, 1973.

Ross, J. E. and M. J. Kami, *Corporate Management in Crisis*, Prentice-Hall, 1973.

Senate Committee on Commerce, *The Penn Central and Other Railroads*, US Government, 1973.

Smith, R. A., *Corporations in Crisis*, Doubleday, 1966.

Westwick, C. A., *How to Use Management Ratios*, Gower Press, 1973.

Index

Printed in Great Britain at the Alden Press, Oxford